Robin Nixon's

PHP

Crash Course

Learn PHP in 14 easy lectures

Robin Nixon's
PHP
Crash Course

Learn PHP in 14 easy lectures

Robin Nixon

 Nixon
Publishing

ROBIN NIXON'S PHP CRASH COURSE

By Robin Nixon

Copyright © 2012 Nixon Publishing, 4 Coast Drive, New Romney, Kent TN28 8NX, UK

Published by: Nixon Publishing
                 4 Coast Drive
                 Greatstone
                 New Romney
                 Kent TN28 8NX
                 United Kingdom

Email: info@nixonpublishing.com
Website: nixonpublishing.com

 ISBN: 978-0956895646

For Julie

About the author

Robin Nixon has been a writer for 30 years, has written in excess of 500 articles for many of the UK's top magazines, and has authored over sixteen books.

Robin started his writing career in the Cheshire homes for disabled people, where he was responsible for setting up computer rooms in a number of residential homes, evaluating and tailoring hardware and software so that disabled people could use the new technology, and writing supporting documentation and articles for a selection of national magazines. After this Robin's career became a hundred percent writing-oriented when he joined a large magazine publisher, where he held a variety of different editorial positions, before leaving to become a self-employed writer.

With the dawn of the Internet in the 1990s, Robin branched out into developing websites (including the world's first licensed Internet radio station). In order to enable people to continue to surf while listening, Robin also developed the first known pop-up windows. In the late 1990s and early 2000s Robin and his family moved to the USA a couple of times, once to run a web design company in California, and then again to set up an English Tearoom in Texas. In between times they ran several successful pubs, bed and breakfasts and nightclubs in England.

In recent years Robin has begun to focus more closely on motivation and personal improvement in his writing, while still continuing to produce more in his popular series of books on computing, which have now been translated into several different languages. Robin lives on the south-east coast of England (where he writes full time), along with his five children and wife Julie (a trained nurse and university lecturer) – between them they also foster three disabled children.

Other web development books by Robin Nixon

- *Learning PHP, MySQL and JavaScript*, O'Reilly 2009
- *HTML5 For iOS And Android*, McGraw-Hill, 2011
- *Robin Nixon's CSS & CSS3 Crash Course*, Nixon, 2011
- *Robin Nixon's HTML & HTML5 Crash Course*, Nixon, 2011
- *Robin Nixon's JavaScript Crash Course*, Nixon, 2012
- *The Web Developer's Cookbook*, McGraw-Hill, 2012
- *Learning PHP, MySQL, JavaScript & CSS (2nd edition)*, O'Reilly 2012

TABLE OF CONTENTS

Lecture 4: PHP Operators 37

Lecture 5: PHP Arrays 57

Lecture 6: Multi-dimensional Arrays 67

Lecture 7: The PHP Array Functions 85

Lecture 8: Controlling Program Flow 109

Lecture 9: Looping Sections of Code 125

Lecture 10: PHP Functions 139

Lecture 11: PHP Objects 155

Lecture 12: Errors and Expressions 171

Lecture 13: Web Forms And Security 185

Lecture 14: Advanced PHP 203

LEARN PHP THE QUICK AND EASY WAY

PHP is the most popular scripting language used in the Internet by far. Being a scripting language means that PHP code is quickly compiled each time it is called, so there is no need for you to compile it yourself. And you lose almost no response time because that compilation occurs in only milliseconds.

Because of this it's extremely easy to make a quick change to a few lines of PHP code, and then instantly see the result of running it. Hence development time is decreased compared with using a compiled language such as C.

There is an alternative scripting language called Perl that used to be the most popular one, but PHP probably leaped to the forefront because (even when it was first released) it ran far more quickly than Perl, and you could run many more instances of a PHP program on a server, saving you on the cost of purchasing additional hardware.

Nowadays Perl is a fast and powerful language too, and you can achieve similar results with both, although PHP remains far and away the most popular choice among web developers.

About This Course

In this course I assume only that you are familiar with basic HTML (and perhaps CSS too), but that you do not have any experience of programming, or have never used PHP before. I also assume that you desire to take your web development to the next level by taking advantage of the dynamic interactivity that PHP provides.

This course therefore starts at the very beginning and takes you through everything you need to know one step at a time, with plenty of useful (and fully tested) examples throughout.

Even if you are a complete novice, after completing this course you will be able to program with PHP and an intermediate level and will be completely comfortable with including PHP scripts in your web pages.

Please remember as you work your way through this course that it is a crash course, and since PHP is a vast language with thousands of functions, it isn't possible to teach you everything in this one course. That said it provides a comprehensive grounding in what I believe are the most important aspects of PHP.

So should you feel I could have written more on a particular subject, please remember that this course takes you to an intermediate level. If you wish to know more, use Google or browse the *php.net* website, and you'll find what you're looking for.

The Example Files

To save you typing them in and to avoid introducing typographical errors, all the examples in this course can be downloaded from the companion website at the following URL. Just click on the *Download Examples* link to retrieve the *examples.zip* archive, which you can extract to obtain all the files, and which are located by lecture into folders:

```
phpcrashcourse.net
```

Thanks And Good Luck

Thanks again for purchasing this book. I hope you find it teaches you everything you want to know, and helps you to the next level in your web development endeavors.

- Robin Nixon

INTRODUCTION TO PHP

By following this lecture you will:

- ✓ *Obtain an overview of what PHP is and how to use it.*
- ✓ *Learn the history of the PHP language.*
- ✓ *Know how to install a PHP server on your computer.*

PHP IS A free scripting language that is provided on most Linux, Unix and BSD systems, or which can easily be installed on them. It is also freely available on both Microsoft Windows PCs, and Apple Mac OS X computers. Therefore, no matter what platform you develop with, there is a version of PHP available for you.

This course is aimed squarely at people who have learned basic HTML (and perhaps a little CSS) but are interested in doing more. For example, you may wish to create more dynamic systems, provide form processing of user-supplied data, support Ajax functionality and more. During this course you'll be shown how to do all these things and much more using PHP.

As you progress it is never assumed that you know anything about a solution, and you are taken through each example step by step with the explanations included, so there is minimal need to look up anything elsewhere. All the examples files from this course are in a ZIP archive, which you can download at the following URL:

```
phpcrashcourse.net/examples.zip
```

A Little History

The PHP programming language was written by Rasmus Lerdorf and it was originally crafted from a set of Perl scripts he combined into what he called his *Personal Home Page* tools, hence the name PHP. These scripts did things like display data such as his résumé, and store and report analytics such as his web page activity. Having started his project in 1994, Lerdorf refined it by rewriting all the scripts in C, compiling them, and then released the result to a Usenet group in 1995. The syntax of PHP was similar to Perl because it was loosely based on that used in the C programming language, and it had much of the same functionality that PHP provides today, with access to variables, form-handling, and embedded HTML.

The Usenet upload was received with enthusiasm and soon a team of developers had assembled who spent the next couple of years extending, improving and testing PHP until they felt it was ready for wider publication in 1997, particularly once Zeev Suraski and Andi Gutmans, a pair of Israeli developers had rewritten the main parser, making it significantly faster and more powerful. They also changed the full name of the program to *PHP: Hypertext Processor*.

Soon after, the Israeli developers started work on rewriting the core engine of PHP, which was called Zend, the same name as a company they founded in Israel. Since then Zend has gone on to release several new versions of PHP, including the free version I recommend you install for this course, *Zend Server Community Edition* (or CE for short). At the time of writing (mid 2012) the most recent version of PHP is version 5.4 and, despite there already being books available for it, PHP 6 has not yet been published. In fact, most of the features slated for version 6 have been incorporated into version 5.4. Therefore it is unlikely that version 6 will be made available for some considerable time. You can keep up-to-date with the latest PHP announcements at *php.net*.

Info for Programmers

If you can already program in another language such as C or Java (for example) you'll find yourself at home with PHP, and here are a few things you should know about the language that will make your learning process even quicker. If you are not a programmer you may skip to the next section as these terms will be explained later in the course.

To begin with, PHP supports much of the structured programming syntax used in C such as `if()` statements, `while()` and `for()` loops, `switch()` statements and so on and, like C, each statement must be terminated with a semicolon.

PHP is a scripting language (so it's not compiled) and, in common with other scripting languages, it uses dynamic typing, in which types are associated with values rather than variables. Values are interpreted as integers, floating point, strings or other types according to the way in why they are used within an expression. This makes PHP easy to use since you don't have to declare the type of a variable, but it can result in unexpected errors in certain instances, unless you force the variable type in a process known as casting.

Being scripted, you can place PHP code within HTML tags to add functionality to basic HTML web pages. In fact you can have as many segments of PHP as you like in a web document, or simply include PHP program files. Unlike C or Java, though, all variables in PHP must be prefaced with a $ symbol, and omitting this symbol is the cause of most syntax errors encountered by beginners to PHP – so make sure you use them.

PHP supports OOP (Object Oriented Programming) and offers private and protected member variables and methods, along with abstract classes, final classes, abstract methods, and final methods. It also uses a standard way of declaring constructors and destructors, similar to that of other object-oriented languages such as C++, and a standard exception handling model.

Why is PHP so Popular?

There are three main reasons for PHP's popularity. Firstly PHP integrates seamlessly with HTML. Even if you know next to no programming it's very easy to rename your *.html* files to *.php* and they will automatically become PHP programs, albeit ones that display themselves as an HTML page.

But then, whenever you need a little dynamic functionality, you can drop in a quick line of PHP code, like the following snippet, for example, which will display the day of the week:

```
<?php echo date("l"); ?>
```

Secondly it's easy to learn. With a few simple PHP function under your belt, almost without knowing it, you're already a PHP programmer. Add in `for()` loops and a couple of other constructs and you can very quickly start making your own dynamic websites.

Thirdly there's excellent support from the PHP programming community and courses such as this; just type "help PHP" into Google and you'll be presented with a staggering 2 billion search results.

Downloading and Installing Web Browsers

If you are going to test your PHP programs thoroughly then you will need to see how they run on all the different browsers currently in use. Following is a list of the five major web browsers and their Internet download locations. While all of them can be installed on a Windows PC, some of them are not available for OS X or Linux. The web pages at these URLs are smart and offer up the correct version to download according to your operating system, if available:

- Apple Safari   `apple.com/safari`
- Google Chrome   `google.com/chrome`
- Microsoft Internet Explorer `microsoft.com/ie`
- Mozilla Firefox   `mozilla.com/firefox`
- Opera   `opera.com/download`

Before proceeding with this book I recommend that you ensure you have installed as many of these browsers on your computer as you can.

If you're running any version of Windows from XP onwards, then you will be able to install all of them, but on other operating systems it's not quite so easy. For example, on Mac OS X, because development of IE for the Mac was halted many years ago when it reached version 5, you can install all the browsers except for Microsoft Internet Explorer.

So your best option on a Mac is to either perform a dual install of Windows alongside OS X, or ensure you have access to a Windows PC. After all, unless you intend to only develop for Mac computers, people using a Windows operating system will represent two thirds of your users.

As for Linux, not only does it not have access to Internet Explorer, there is no version of Safari either, although all the other browsers do come in Linux flavors. And, as with OS X, while various solutions exist that incorporate Wine for running Internet Explorer, they only seem to work with some distributions and not others, so it can be a bit of a minefield trying to find a bulletproof way for you to run Windows browsers on Linux.

What it all comes down to is that, if you will be developing on a non-Windows computer I recommend that you arrange to have access to a Windows PC, or have Windows installed as a dual boot (or a virtual machine) alongside your main operating system, so that you can fully test your programs before publishing them to the web at large.

Note: *Don't forget that nowadays you also need to check your projects on iOS and/or Android phones and/or tablets if you are also targeting that market. For this you really will need access to at least an iPhone 3Gs and an iPad 1, as well as a decent Android phone and tablet. And with Microsoft now pushing the Metro front end to both Windows Phone 7 and Windows 8, it seems likely that you will also want to arrange access to a Windows Phone, and also a tablet that runs Windows 8.*

Choosing a Program Editor

Long gone are the days of relying on a simple text editor for coding, because software for writing program code has progressed in leaps and bounds in recent years, with text editors having been replaced by powerful program editors that highlight your syntax using different colors, and which can quickly locate things for you like matching (and missing) brackets and braces, and so on.

Following is a list of free program editors (including the platforms they run on and download URLs) that will all do a great job of helping you to write code quickly and efficiently. Which one you choose is largely down to personal preference – in my case I have settled on Notepad++:

- Bluefish   Lin/Mac   `bluefish.openoffice.nl`
- Cream   Lin/Win   `cream.sourceforge.net`
- Editra   Lin/Mac/Win   `editra.org`
- Free HTML Editor Win   `coffeecup.com/free-editor`
- jEdit   Lin/Mac/Win   `jedit.org`
- Notepad++   Win   `notepad-plus.sourceforge.net`

When using a program editor you will usually find that by moving the cursor to different parts of a program you can highlight sections of the code. For example, placing the cursor next to any bracket in Notepad++ automatically highlights the matching one.

Program editors also commonly support multiple tabs, folding away sections of code that aren't being worked on, multiple views into the same document, search and replace across multiple documents and so on, These are all features that you would miss once you grow used to using them.

Installing a PHP Server

If you wish to test your code on a local development computer before uploading it to a web server elsewhere, you'll need to install a web server and PHP processor. This means you can instantly try out any code changes you make without having to upload them to the internet first, speeding up the development process.

Installing a PHP web server is relatively simple because the developers of PHP have released an all-in-one application called *Zend Server Community Edition* (or CE for short) that includes all of PHP, an Apache web server and a MySQL database (if you use a custom install and check the box), and which you can download from the following URL:

```
zend.com/products/server-ce
```

Versions are available for all three main operating systems (Windows, Mac OS X and Linux), and the installation process is reasonably straight forward, although you'll need to carefully read the prompts you are given and make intelligent responses to them.

The place where you will store all your PHP files and from where they will run is known as the server's *document root*, and you will need to know where this is. Following is a list of default locations for document root that Zend Server CE creates on different operating systems. If you keep your various HTML, JavaScript and PHP files in that folder (and subfolders), then they can all be served up by the Apache web server:

- Windows   `C:/Program Files/Zend/Apache2/htdocs`
- Mac OS X   `/usr/local/zend/apache2/htdocs`
- Debian/Ubuntu Linux   `/var/www`
- Fedora Linux   `/var/www/html`
- Generic Linux   `/usr/local/zend/apache2/htdocs`

Unfortunately there's no room to go into further details about Zend Server CE in this course, but there is a very good online user guide, which you can access at the following URL:

```
tinyurl.com/usingzendce
```

Summary

OK. With all of that preamble and introduction out of the way you should be ready to start out on this crash course, beginning with the following lecture which explains how to incorporate PHP code within a web page.

INCORPORATING PHP CODE INTO A WEB PAGE

By following this lecture you will:

- ✓ *Learn how to use single and multi-line comments..*
- ✓ *Understand the purpose of semicolons.*
- ✓ *Know how to include PHP in your web pages.*

THE WHOLE POINT of PHP is that it is designed to offer dynamic functionality to what previously were static web pages. Therefore PHP code is generally embedded within a web page to which it applies.

This can be in the form of the direct code itself, or by means of a tag that tells the browser the location of a file containing some PHP to load in and execute. This external file may be on the same or a different web server.

Additionally, the location within a web page at which you insert the PHP (or link to a PHP file) becomes the location in which any output from the PHP will be inserted.

Therefore, for this and other reasons, where you place your PHP can be important. So I'll begin this course by looking at how and where you should include PHP in your web pages.

Where to Place the PHP Code

It can make a difference where you place your PHP code. For example, if you wish default output to go straight into the current document's body, you may choose to place your PHP somewhere directly within the `<body>` and `</body>` tags. On the other hand, if you wish to be able to output HTML within the head of a document, you might choose to place your PHP code within the `<head>` and `</head>` tags. Or you might place *all* your HTML output within a PHP script, outputting it from built-in functions.

In the Document Head

To insert your PHP within the head of a document you must place `<?php` and `?>` tags where the script is to go, like this (highlighted in bold text):

```
<html>
  <head>
    <title>Page Title</title>
    <?php
      // Your PHP goes here
    ?>
  </head>
  <body>
    The document body goes here
  </body>
</html>
```

In the Document Body

To insert your PHP within the body of a document you must place `<?php` and `?>` tags where the script is to go, like this (highlighted in bold text):

```
<html>
  <head>
    <title>Page Title</title>
  </head>
```

```
<body>
   The document body goes here
   <?php
     // Your PHP goes here
   ?>
</body>
</html>
```

Including PHP Files

If you wish to keep your PHP code separate from your document contents (something you are likely to want to do once your PHP starts to become any length other than small), you can place it in its own file (usually with the file extension *.php*) and, instead of inserting lines of code between <?php and ?> tags, you would simple place an include() function call, like this (highlighted in bold text):

```
<html>
   <head>
      <title>Page Title</title>
      <?php
        include('myscript.php');
      ?>
   </head>
   <body>
      The document body goes here
   </body>
</html>
```

If the script file is not in the current directory you must include the path along with the filename, like this:

```
<?php include('pathtofolder/myscript.php'); ?>
```

Note: See how the code has been compressed into a single line here, which is purely a matter of personal choice, but probably a good idea for something as simple as an `include()` call.

If the code is on another server, include the correct `http://` (or `https://` prefix, domain and path) like this:

```php
<?php include('http://server.com/folder/myscript.php'); ?>
```

When including a script, rather than embedding it in the head of a document, you may choose to place it into the body instead, like this:

```html
<html>
  <head>
    <title>Page Title</title>
  </head>
  <body>
    <?php include('myscript.php'); ?>
    The document body goes here
  </body>
</html>
```

Using `require()`

When you issue an `include()` call, if the file to include is not found no error will be displayed but because the file is not included your page may not display correctly. To cater for this possibility you can use the alternative `require()` function, which will issue an error if the file is not found, like this:

```php
<?php require('myscript.php'); ?>
```

Using `include_once()` and `require_once()`

Sometimes you wish to have a script included *only once* in a web page, and you can do this by adding the suffix `_once` to either the `include()` or `require()` call, like this:

```
<?php include_once('myscript.php'); ?>
<?php require_once('myscript.php'); ?>
```

In either case, if the file has already been included into the current document, the statement will be ignored so that the file is not included again. Otherwise the file will be included if it exists. If it doesn't exist no error will be given if you use `include_once()`, but you will receive an error when using `require_once()`.

Using Comments

Before looking at the PHP language and its syntax in the following lecture, I want to first introduce the commenting feature. Using comments you can add text to a PHP program that explains what it does. This will help you later when you are debugging, and is especially helpful when other people have to maintain code that you write.

There are two ways to create a comment in PHP, the first of which is to preface it with two slashes, as follows:

```
// This is a comment
```

You can also place a comment after a PHP statement, like the following, which assigns a value to a variable (remember that PHP variables begin with a $ symbol):

```
$anumber = 42; // Assigns 42 to $anumber
```

Or, if you wish to temporarily prevent a line of code from executing, you can insert a comment tag before it, and the statement will be completely ignored, like this:

```
// $anumber = 42;
```

Sometimes you need to be able to comment out more than a single line of text. In which case you can use the multi-line form of commenting in which you start the comment with /*, and end it with */, like this:

```
/* This is a multi-line
   set of comments, which
```

```
can appear over any

number of lines      */
```

Note: As well as supporting extensive documentation, this form of commenting lets you temporarily comment out complete blocks of code by simply placing the start and end comment tags as required – something that can be extremely helpful when debugging.

Using Semicolons

You must add a semicolon after every PHP statement, and can place more than one statement on a single line, as long as you separate them with a semicolon. So, for example, the three following sets of code are all valid syntax:

```
$a = 1;
$b = 2;
$a = 1; $b = 2;
```

However, none of the following are valid, as PHP will not know how to make sense of anything due to the omission of semicolons:

```
$a = 1
$b = 2
$a = 1 $b = 2
```

Note: Think of the semicolon as acting like a command that tells PHP it has reached the end of a statement and can now process it. You do not, however, have to place semicolons at the end of lines that are commented out.

Summary

Now that you know how and where to put PHP in your web pages and have a basic understanding of how to create a PHP statement or comment, in the following lecture I'll begin to explain the syntax of the language.

PHP LANGUAGE SYNTAX

By following this lecture you will:

- ✓ *Learn about case sensitivity.*
- ✓ *Understand the use of whitespace characters.*
- ✓ *Know how to use variables to store values.*

I'VE ALREADY DISCUSSED some of the *syntax* used by the PHP language, such as how to comment out sections of code, and how semicolons must be used after each statement. But what is meant by syntax? Well, it's a set of rules that define how to correctly structure a PHP program.

In this section I'll outline the major syntax issues so that when you start programming you'll introduce the minimum of errors, so please forgive me if there's a little overlap with earlier sections.

Case Sensitivity

PHP is what is known as a case-sensitive language. This means that it distinguishes between the use of the upper and lower case letters `a-z` and `A-Z`.

So, for example, the variable `$MyVariable` is quite different from `$myvariable` (variables being special names used to stand in for values such as numbers or strings of characters, explained a little further on).

PHP will treat these as two totally different variables so you need to be careful when choosing your variable names. Generally I observe the following guidelines so that I can more easily go back and understand code I may have written some time in the past:

- All global variables that are accessible anywhere in a program are set to all uppercase, such as `$HIGHSCORE`.
- Temporary variables used in loops are single letters in lower case, such as `$j`.

This is only the formatting that I use, and you may choose to apply different upper and lower case rules to this, or simply stick to all lower case, it's entirely up to you.

Whitespace

Any spaces and tabs are known as *whitespace*, and any combination of these is usually treated by PHP as if it were a single space. The exception is when they are placed inside quotation marks, in which case they form part of a string, and all the characters are used.

Newline or carriage return characters are also treated as whitespace by PHP (unless within quotes). Therefore, for example, the statement `$a = $b + $c;` is valid on a single line, but you may also format it in the following manner, which illustrates one reason for PHP requiring semicolons (to allow you to split long statements across multiple lines):

```
$a = $b
+ $c;
```

Variables

A variable in any programming language is simply a container for a value. For example, imagine that you have a few empty plastic pots, into which you can place items (see Figure 3-1). Think of these as a metaphor for variables, in that you can take a small piece of paper and write the number 42 (for example) on it and insert it into one of the pots. If you then take a marker pen and write `$MyVariable` on the pot, it is just like a PHP variable being set using this line of code:

```
$MyVariable = 42;
```

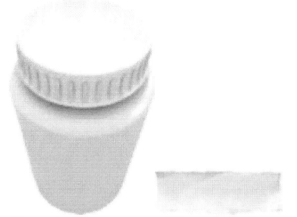

Figure 1: An empty pot and blank piece of paper.

Figure 3-2 shows the pot now labeled and the paper written on. You can now manipulate this variable in a variety of ways. For example, you can add another value to it, like this:

```
$MyVariable = $MyVariable + 13;
```

This has the effect of adding 13 to the value of 42 already stored in the variable so that the result is 55, the new value held in the variable. This is analogous to taking the piece of paper with the number 42 written on it out of the pot labeled $MyVariable, noting the value, adding 13 to it, and then replacing that piece of paper with another on which you have written the number 55 (see Figure 3-3), which you then place back into the pot.

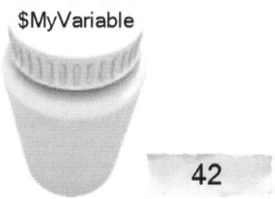

Figure 2: The pot has been labeled, and paper written on.

Figure 3: A new slip of paper with the number 55 on it.

Likewise you might issue the following command (for example), which will multiply the current value in the variable (`55`) by `3`:

```
$MyVariable = $MyVariable * 3;
```

Again, this is equivalent to taking the paper from the pot, performing the multiplication, and placing a new piece of paper with the result of `165` (see Figure 3-4) back into the pot. All the time the current numeric value is updated and popped inside the pot with the label `$MyVariable` on it, so that any time that value needs to be referenced (looked up), the pot can simply be opened and the slip of paper inside then read.

Variable Naming

There are a number of rules governing how you use the PHP programming language. For instance variables must begin with a `$` symbol, which should be followed by either an upper or lower case letter (`a-z` or `A-Z`).

After the first letter, variables can contain upper or lower case letters, digits (`0-9`) or the `_` symbol. Variables may not contain any mathematical operators (such as `+` or `*`), punctuation (such as `!` or `&`), or spaces.

String Variables

When a variable is used to store a number (as in the preceding examples) it's known as a *numeric variable*. However, it's also possible to store text in a variable, in which case the variable is called a *string variable* (since sequences of characters are called strings in programming languages).

Figure 4: Another piece of paper with the number 165 on it.

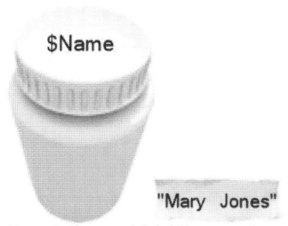

Figure 5: This pot is labeled "$Name" and contains a string value.

Examples of strings include the name `"Bill Smith"`, the sequence of characters `"A23bQ%j"` and even the characters `"123"` which, in this case are a string of digits, not the number `123`.

In the same way that you can store a number in a variable, so you can a string, and you use the same method of assignment, like this:

```
$Name = "Mary Jones";
```

Notice the use of double quotation marks around this string. These are what tell PHP that the value is a string, and is how you can assign the string `"123"` to a variable, as opposed to the number `123`, for example. In terms of the pot and paper metaphor, the preceding statement is equivalent to labeling a new pot as `"$Name"` and writing `"Mary Jones"` on a piece of paper that you place in it, as shown in Figure 3-5.

Obviously you can't perform arithmetic on strings, but there are other actions you can take such as shortening them, adding more characters to the front, middle or end, extracting a portion of a string, and more. For example, you can concatenate two strings together (attach one to the other) using the `.` operator, like this:

```
$Singer = "Paul";
$Singer = Singer . " Simon";
```

The result of these two statements is to concatenate the string "Paul" (first assigned to, and then read from the variable $Singer) with the string " Simon" and place the resulting string back into the variable $Singer. In Lecture 6 I'll show you the other operations you can perform on strings.

Using Quotation Marks in Strings

You have seen the use of the double quote character to indicate the start and end of a string, but you may also use the single quote if you prefer, like this:

```
$Dinner = 'Fish and Chips';
```

The end result is almost identical, whichever type of quotation marks you use (I say almost because there is a subtle difference explained a little further on, in the section *Embedding Variables Within a String*).

But there is a good reason why you may choose one type instead of the other, and that's when you need to include a particular quotation mark within a string. For example, suppose you needed to store the string "Isn't the weather fine?". As it stands, using double quotation marks works just fine, but what would happen if you surrounded the string with single quotation marks instead, like this: 'Isn't the weather fine?'?

Well, you would get a syntax error because PHP would see only the string 'Isn' and then some gibberish following it, like this: t the weather fine?'. Then again what about the string 'Jane said, "Hello"'? This time, using single quotes this string works but, because of the double quotes within it, if you were to surround the string with double quotes like this, "Jane said, "Hello"", PHP would see one string, like this: "Jane said, ", some gibberish (to PHP) like this: Hello, and another string with nothing in it, like this: "". It would give up at all this and generate an error.

Note: Placing a pair of quotes together with nothing between them results in what is called the empty string. *It is commonly used for erasing or initializing the value of a string variable.*

Using Heredoc Strings

There's another way you can create a string in PHP that removes the need to surround it in quotation marks of any kind, and that's to use a *Heredoc* construct, like this:

```
$tobeornottobe = <<<_EOT

To be, or not to be, that is the question:

Whether 'tis Nobler in the mind to suffer

The Slings and Arrows of outrageous Fortune,

Or to take Arms against a Sea of troubles,

And by opposing end them: to die, to sleep

_EOT;
```

Heredoc text behaves just like a double-quoted string, but without needing the double quotes. This means that no quotes of either types in a Heredoc need to be escaped (but the escape codes listed in the following section can still be used).

The value _EOT is an identifier that marks the start and end of a Heredoc string, and it follows the same naming rules for any PHP label. However, a convention for heredocs is to preface them with an underscore, and to use only capital letters, so I generally use _EOT (for End Of Text) so I can always find all my Heredoc strings with a quick search.

Note: You must be careful when using a Heredoc because the exact token following the <<< must appear at the start of the line following the Heredoc text. It must also end with a semicolon. If there is no semicolon, or the Heredoc identifier is not the first thing on a line, the Heredoc will fall through to the end of the script (and therefore be unterminated), resulting in nasty errors.

Escaping Characters

But things can get more interesting, because what about the occasions when you might require both types of quote to be included within a string, like this: `"Mark said, "I can't wait""`? As it stands this string will cause a syntax error, but you can easily fix it using the escape character, which is simply a backslash, like this: `"Mark said, \"I can't wait\""`.

What the escape character does is tell PHP to ignore the \ character and to use the character following it as a string element, and not a string container.

You may escape either of the quotation marks inside a string to ensure they are used only as string elements, and can also use escape characters to insert other characters that you cannot easily type in such as tabs and newlines, as follows:

- \' single quote
- \" double quote
- \\ backslash
- \b backspace
- \f form feed
- \n new line
- \r carriage return
- \t tab

Embedding Variables Within a String

One of PHP's more powerful features is the ability to embed a variable name inside a string, which will then be replaced with the variable's value. For example, the following code creates two variables and then embeds them in a string variable.

```
$age    = "52";

$name   = "Robin"

$string = "My name is $name and I am $age";
```

The result is that $string will now contain the value "My name is Robin and I am 52". To embed variables within strings, the strings must be surrounded with double quotes. If you use single quotes the exact contents of the string will be used and no variable values will be substituted.

For example, the following results in $string only containing the value "My name is $name and I am $age":

```
$age    = "52";

$name   = "Robin"

$string = 'My name is $name and I am $age';
```

You may also place variables within Heredoc strings too, since they behave like double-quoted strings.

Note: Now you see another reason for PHP requiring that variables begin with a $ symbol; it supports the ability to embed them in strings.

Variable Typing and Casting

In PHP, unlike some other programming languages, a variable can change its type automatically. For example a string can become a number, and vice versa, according to the way in which the variable is referenced. For example, take the following assignment in which the variable $MyVar is given the string value of "12345":

```
$MyVar = "12345";
```

Although the string is created from a group of all digits, it is a string. However, PHP is smart enough to understand that sometimes a string can be a number, so in the following assignment it converts the string value in $MyVar to a number prior to applying the subtraction, and then the resulting value (which is now the number 12000) is stored back in $MyVar, which is now a numeric variable:

```
$MyVar = $MyVar - 345;
```

Likewise, a number can be automatically converted to a string, as in the following two lines, which first set the numeric variable $Time to the value 6, then the string "O'clock" is appended to the number, which is first turned into a string (using the . symbol, which is the string concatenation operator) to make this string concatenation possible:

```
$Time = 6;
$Time = $Time . " O'clock";
```

The result is that $Time is now a string variable with the value "6 O'clock".

Because of this changing of variables from one type to another (known as automatic type casting) it is not actually correct to think of PHP variables in terms of type, so I will no-longer do so. Instead you should consider only their contents and how PHP will interpret them.

However, sometimes it is necessary for you to force the type of a variable and you can do this with PHP's cast operators, as follows:

- (int) or (integer) Cast to an integer
- (bool) or (boolean) Cast to a Boolean value

- (float) or (double) or (real) Cast to a floating point number
- (string) Cast to a string
- (array) Cast to an array
- (object) Cast to an object
- (unset) Cast to NULL (Since PHP 5)

For example, consider the following statement and ask yourself what you think PHP should do with it:

```
$MyVar = (int) "12345";
```

The answer is that the string value is turned into an integer before being assigned to the variable. Likewise you can use a cast like the following to turn a number into a string:

```
$MyVar = (string) 12345;
```

Or you can use the facility to embed a variable within a double-quoted string (or Heredoc) to turn it into a string, like this:

```
$MyNum = 12345;
$MyVar = "$MyNum";
```

Note: Generally the occasions on which you will find it beneficial to use casting are when dealing with values over which you have less control, such as user input that you are processing.

Constants

Constants are similar to variables, in that they store values to be accessed later. However these values remain constant once defined (as you might expect), and cannot be changed.

You define a constant like this:

```
define('SITE_NAME', 'ACME Products Web Store');
```

Then, to read the contents of the variable you just refer to it like a regular variable (without preceding it with a dollar symbol):

```
echo SITE_NAME;
```

Predefined Constants

PHP comes ready made with dozens of predefined constants that you generally will be unlikely to use as a beginner to PHP. However there are a few known as the *magic constants* which you will find useful. They start and end with a pair of underscore characters and are detailed following:

- `__LINE__` The current line number of the file.
- `__FILE__` The full path and filename of the file. If used inside an include, the name of the included file is returned. `__FILE__` always contains an absolute path with symbolic links resolved whereas in older versions it contained relative path under some circumstances.
- `__DIR__` The directory of the file. If used inside an include, the directory of the included file is returned. This is equivalent to `dirname(__FILE__)`. The directory name does not have a trailing slash unless it is the root directory.
- `__FUNCTION__` Returns the function name as it was declared (case-sensitive). In PHP 4 its value is always lowercased.
- `__CLASS__` Returns the class name as it was declared. In PHP 4 its value is always lowercased.
- `__METHOD__` Returns the method name as it was declared.
- `__NAMESPACE__` The name of the current namespace. This constant is defined in compile-time.

One handy use of these variables is for debugging purposes when you need to insert a line of code to see if program flow reaches it:

```
echo "This is line " . __LINE__ " of file " . __FILE__;
```

In the above case the current program line in the current file (including the path) being executed is output to the web browser.

The `echo` and `print` commands

Having just used the `echo` command in the previous example I should now explain it. The `echo` command can be used in a number of different ways to output text from the server to your browser. Simply place a variable or literal value (such as a string or number) after the echo command, and the contents of the variable or the literal value will be output to the browser.

There is also an alternative to echo that you can use and that is print. These commands are quite similar to each other with the exception that print is an actual PHP function and will only take a single parameter, whereas echo is only a PHP language construct.

By and large the echo command will be a tad faster than print in general text output because, not being a function, it doesn't set a return value. On the other hand, because it isn't a function, echo cannot be used as part of a more complex expression, while print can. Here's an example to output whether the value of a variable is TRUE or FALSE using print, something you could not perform in the same manner with echo.

```
$var ? print "true" : print "false";
```

As you will learn in a Lecture 4, the question mark is being used here as the *ternary operator*, to test the variable $var for being TRUE or FALSE. Whichever command is on the left of the following colon is executed upon $var being TRUE, while the command to the right is executed upon $var being FALSE.

Superglobal Variables

Starting with PHP 4.1.0 there are several predefined variables available. These are known as superglobal variables, which means they are accessible absolutely everywhere in a PHP program.

These superglobals contain lots of useful information about the currently running program and its environment, as follows:

- $GLOBALS[] An associative array containing references to all variables that are currently defined in the global scope of the script. The variable names are the keys of the array. See Lecture 10 for more details.
- $_SERVER[] An array containing information such as headers, paths, and script locations. The entries in this array are created by the web server and there is no guarantee that every web server will provide any or all of these.
- $_GET[] An associative array of variables passed to the current script via the HTTP Get method.

- `$_POST[]` An associative array of variables passed to the current script via the HTTP Post method.
- `$_FILES[]` An associative array of items uploaded to the current script via the HTTP Post method.
- `$_COOKIE[]` An associative array of variables passed to the current script via HTTP Cookies.
- `$_SESSION[]` An associative array containing session variables available to the current script.
- `$_REQUEST[]` An associative array that by default contains the contents of `$_GET`, `$_POST` and `$_COOKIE`.
- `$_ENV[]` An associative array of variables passed to the current script via the environment method.

To illustrate how you use them, among the various pieces of information supplied by superglobal variables is the URL of the page which referred the user to the current web page. This referring page information can be accessed like this:

```
$came_from = $_SERVER['HTTP_REFERER'];
```

If the user came from another (referring) page, its details will be saved in `$came_from`, otherwise if the user came straight to your web page, for example by typing its URL directly into a browser, then `$came_from` will simply be set to an empty string.

Superglobals and Security

A word of caution is in order before you start using superglobal variables because they are often used by hackers trying to find exploits to break into your website. What they do is load up `$_POST`, `$_GET` or other superglobals with malicious code they hope you will not pre-define, such as Unix or MySQL commands.

Therefore you should always sanitize these variables before using them. As you will learn more about in Lecture 13, one way to do this is via the PHP `htmlentities()` function. What it does is convert all characters into HTML entities. For example, the less-than and greater-than characters (< and >) are transformed into the strings `&lt;` and `&gt;` so that they are rendered harmless, as are all quotes, backslashes and so on.

Therefore a much better way to access `$_SERVER` (and other superglobals) is:

```
$came_from = htmlentities($_SERVER['HTTP_REFERER']);
```

Summary

Don't worry if you are not clear about some of the subjects covered here such as arrays, functions and superglobals, as they will be explained as you progress through this course. However, we've actually covered quite a lot of ground in this lecture, which has explained some of the simpler PHP syntax and data handling capabilities. In the following lecture we'll start to see how these come together with operators to enable you to start creating simple PHP expressions.

PHP OPERATORS

By following this lecture you will:

- ✓ *Be able to use operators effectively.*
- ✓ *Know how to combine assignments with operators.*
- ✓ *Understand the reason for operator precedence.*

IN THE PREVIOUS lecture you saw a few examples of operators in action, such as the + sign used for addition, the . for concatenating strings together, the – sign used for subtraction, and the = operator used for assigning values.

But PHP supports many more operators than that, such as *, / and more, and also includes functions you can draw on for more advanced expression evaluation, such as `sin()`, `sqrt()`, and many others. In this lecture I'll explain all of these, how they work and how to use them.

This is an important lecture since it covers much of the foundation of how PHP works so, even if you have programmed before using another language, I recommend you read this thoroughly, because there are a number of things PHP handles in a unique manner.

Arithmetic Operators

The arithmetic operators in PHP are the ones that allow you to create numeric expressions and there are more than simply addition, subtraction, multiplication and division, as shown in Table 4-1.

Operator	Description	Example	Result
+	Addition	3 + 11	14
–	Subtraction	9 – 4	5
*	Multiplication	3 * 4	12
/	Division	21 / 7	3
%	Modulus (*remainder after division*)	21 % 8	5
++	Increment	$a = 5; ++$a	($a *equals*) 6
––	Decrement	$a = 5; ––$a	($a *equals*) 4

Table 1: The arithmetic operators.

You can try these operators out for yourself by loading the file *math_operators.php* from the companion archive into a browser, which should look like Figure 4-1. Try changing the various values and operators applied, and check the results you get.

The first four of these operators should be very clear to you so I'll only explain the last three, starting with the modulus operator, %. What this operator returns is simply the remainder after calculating a division. For example, the modulus of 12 and 4, calculated using the expression 12 % 4, is 0, because 4 goes into 12 an exact number of times, and therefore there is no remainder.

On the other hand, the modulus of 24 and 5 (calculated as 24 % 5) is 4, because 5 goes into 24 four times (5 × 4 is 20), leaving a remainder of 4, the modulus of the expression.

Now let's look at the increment and decrement operators. These come in tremendously handy because without them you would have to write expressions like this:

```
$a = $a + 1;
```

This is cumbersome when you only want to increment (or decrement) a value by 1, and so the creators of PHP allow you to use the following syntax instead:

```
++$a;
```

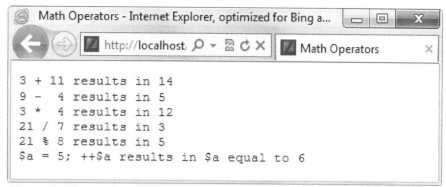

Figure 1: The arithmetic operators in use.

I'm sure you will agree this is much shorter and sweeter. It also comes with fringe benefits too, because the increment and decrement operators can be used within flow control commands such as `if()` statements (which I explain in full detail in Lecture 8, but will give you a taster here).

Consider the following code, which assumes that `$Time` contains a 24-hour time value between `0` and `23`, and which is set up to trigger once an hour, on the hour (using code not shown here, but which is assumed to be in place):

```
$Time = $Time + 1;
echo "The time is $Time";


if ($Time < 12) echo('AM');
else            echo('PM');
```

This code first increments the value in `$Time` by 1, because this code has been called on the hour, so it's now one hour since the last time it was called, and so `$Time` must be updated. Then on the next line it displays the time in the browser, prefaced by the string `'The time is '`.

After that an `if()` statement is reached which tests the variable `$Time` to see whether it currently has a value of less than `12`. If so then it must still be the morning and so the string `'AM'` is output. Otherwise it's the afternoon and so `'PM'` is displayed – fairly straight-forward stuff.

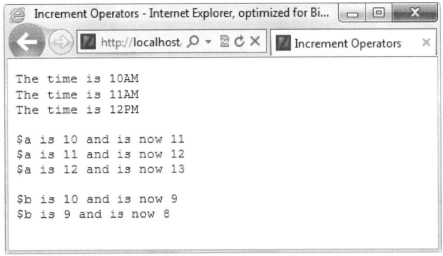

Figure 2: Using the increment operator.

Note: *This is a simple version of the* if() *statement in that it has only a single statement after the* if()*, and there is also only a single one after* else*. Therefore no curly braces are used to enclose the action statements. Please see Lecture 8 for more details on using* if() and else *with multi-statement actions.*

However programmers always like to write the tightest and cleanest code possible, and so the following code is considered better programming practice, as it removes an entire line of code, like this (with the incremented variable and operator highlighted):

```
echo 'The time is ' . ++$Time;


if ($Time < 12) echo 'AM';
else            echo 'PM';
```

Or, even more succinctly, using the ternary operator:

```
echo 'The time is ' . ++$Time;


echo ($Time < 12) ? 'AM' : 'PM';
```

Pre-Incrementing

What has occurred in the previous example is an instance of *pre-incrementing* the variable $Time. In other words, before the value in $Time is used it is incremented. Only after this incrementing is the current value in $Time used for displaying in the echo statement.

In Figure 4-2 these lines of code have been called three times, with an original starting value for $Time of 9 (using the file *inc_and_dec.php* from the companion archive).

Post-Incrementing

You may also place the ++ increment operator after a variable name, and then it is known as *post-incrementing*. What happens when you do this is that the value in the variable being incremented is looked up before the increment, and that value is used by the code accessing it. Only after this value has been looked up is the variable incremented.

The following code illustrates this type of incrementing by displaying both the before and after values in the variable $a (with instances of the variable and increment operator highlighted):

```
echo '$a was ' . $a++ . ' and is now ' . $a)
```

Working through this statement from left to right, first the string '$a was ' is output, then $a++ is displayed. This results in the current value of $a being displayed, and only then is $a incremented. After this the string ' and is now ' is output, followed by the new value in $a, which now contains the incremented value from the earlier increment operation. So, if $a had an initial value of 10, then the following is displayed:

```
$a was 10 and is now 11
```

Pre- and Post-Decrementing

You can use the decrement operator in exactly the same way as the increment operator, and it can either be placed before a variable for pre-incrementing, or after for post-decrementing. Following are two examples that both display the same but achieve the result using pre-decrementing for the first, and post-decrementing for the second (with instances of the variable and decrement operator highlighted):

```
echo '$b was ' . $b    . ' and is now ' . --$b)
echo '$b was ' . $b-- . ' and is now ' .    $b)
```

Here, if $b had an initial value of 10, then the following is displayed:

    $b was 10 and is now 9
    $b was 9 and is now 8

Note: If it's still not entirely clear which type of increment or decrement operator to use out of pre- and post- methods, don't worry, just use the pre- methods (with the operator before the variable) for now, because it will become obvious to you when the time comes that you actually have a need to use the post- method (with the operator after the variable).

Arithmetic Functions

To accompany the arithmetic operators, PHP comes with a math library of functions you can call on, among which are the following:

- abs($a) Returns $a as a positive number.
- acos($a) Returns the arc cosine of $a.
- asin($a) Returns the arc sine of $a.
- atan($a) Returns the arc tangent of $a.
- atan2($a, $b) Returns the arc tangent of $a / $b.
- ceil($a) Rounds up to return the integer closest to $a.
- cos($a) Returns the cosine of $a.
- exp($a) Returns the exponent of $a (E to the power $a).
- floor($a) Rounds down to return the integer closest to $a.
- log($a) Returns the log of $a base E.
- max($a, $b) Returns the maximum of $a and $b.
- min($a, $b) Returns the minimum of $a and $b.
- pow($a, $b) Returns $a to the power $b.
- rand($a, $b) Returns a random number between $a and $b inclusive.
- round($a) Rounds up or down to return the integer closest to $a.
- sin($a) Returns the sine of $a.
- sqrt($a) Returns the square root of $a.
- tan($a) Returns the tangent of $a.

Operator	Description	Example	Result in a
=	Simple Assignment	$a = 42	42
+=	With Addition	$a += 5	26
-=	With Subtraction	$a -= 2	19
*=	With Multiplication	$a *= 3	63
/=	With Division	$a /= 10	2.1
%=	With Modulus	$a %= 4	1

Table 2: The assignment operators.

You should be familiar with most of these, for example, to return the square root of 64 you would use the following:

```
sqrt(64); // Returns 8
```

But there are a couple that need a little more explaining, such as abs(). What this does is take any value (negative, zero or positive), and if it is negative turns in into a positive value, like this:

```
abs(27); // Returns 27
abs(0);  // Returns 0
abs(-5); // Returns 5
```

The other function possibly needing extra explanation is rand(). This returns a statistically random number (although not truly random) between (and including) the two values supplied. So, for example, if you wish to emulate a 12-sided dice you might call it this way:

```
rand(1, 12); // Returns a number between 1 and 12
```

There are many other math functions available in PHP, and you can see the whole list at the following URL:

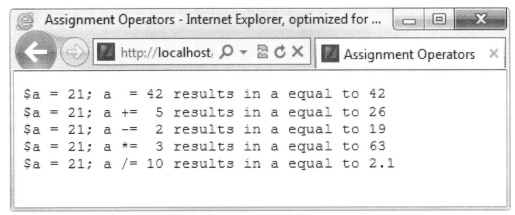

Figure 3: Using the various assignment operators.

`php.net/manual/en/ref.math.php`

Assignment Operators

Like many other languages PHP likes to help you out by offering more efficient ways to achieve results. One of these ways is by letting you combine assignment and arithmetic operators together into six different types of assignment operator. This typically saves lines of code and makes your program code much easier to write, and for others to understand.

Table 4-2 lists the assignment operators available, provides examples of them in use and shows the result of doing so when the variable $a already contains the value 21. You can see the result of using the expressions in this table in Figure 4-3, created with the example file *assignment_operators.php* from the accompanying archive.

So, for example, instead of using $a = $a + 5, you can use the more compact $a += 5. And you can use assignment operators in conjunction with other expressions and variables, as with the following example, which results in a having a value of 15 (10 + (25 / 5)):

```
$a  = 10;
$b  = 25;
$a += ($b / 5);
```

Operator	Description	Example	Result
==	Equal to	1 == 1	TRUE
===	Equal in value & type	1 === '1'	FALSE
!=	Not equal to	1 != 2	TRUE
!==	Not equal in value & type	1 !== '1'	TRUE
>	Greater than	1 > 2	FALSE
<	Less than	1 < 2	TRUE
>=	Greater than or equal to	1 >= 1	TRUE
<=	Less than or equal to	2 <= 1	FALSE

Table 3: The comparison operators.

Comparison Operators

One of the most important process that happens in a program is comparison. For example, possibly the most frequent type of construct used goes along the lines of *if this then do that*.

The job of comparison operators is to figure out the *this* part, and there are eight of them, as listed in Table 4-3.

Figure 4-4 shows several different comparison operators used on different values and the results obtained. It was created using the file *comparison_operators.php*, available in the companion archive.

If you haven't programmed before, some of these operators may seem a little confusing, especially seeing as we are taught as children that = is the *equal-to operator*.

However, in programming languages such as PHP the = is used as an *assignment operator*.

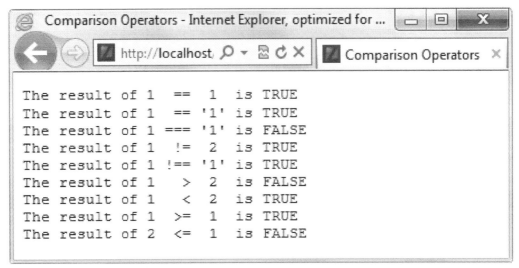

Figure 4: A selection of comparison operators in use.

Therefore code would become harder to read (and the writers of programming languages would have a much harder time figuring out its meaning) if the = symbol were also used to make comparisons. And so the == operator is used for comparisons instead, like this:

```
if ($a == 12) // Do something
```

In PHP, however, the types of variables are loosely defined and it's quite normal, for example, to ask whether 1 is the same as '1', because the string '1' can be used either as a string or as a number depending on the context. Therefore the following expression will return the value TRUE:

```
if (1 == '1') // Results in the value TRUE
```

Note: PHP uses the internal values of TRUE and FALSE to represent the result of making comparisons such as the preceding, and you can use the keywords TRUE and FALSE in your programming to check for these values.

Progressing through the list of comparison operators, when you wish to determine whether two values are the same value and *also* of the same type, you can use the === operator, like this:

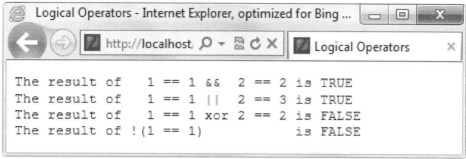

Figure 5: Using logical operators.

```
if (1 === '1') // Results in the value FALSE
```

Similarly you can test whether values are *not* equal (but not comparing the type) using the != operator, like this:

```
if (1 != 2)   // Results in the value TRUE
if (1 != '1') // Results in the value FALSE
```

And if you wish to check whether two values are not equal in *both* value and type you use the !== operator, like this:

```
if (1 !== '1') // Results in the value TRUE
```

The remaining comparison operators test whether one value is greater than, less than, greater than or equal to, or less than or equal to another, like this:

```
if (1 > 2)  // Results in the value FALSE
if (1 < 2)  // Results in the value TRUE
if (1 >= 1) // Results in the value TRUE
if (2 <= 1) // Results in the value FALSE
```

Logical Operators

PHP supports three logical operators with which you can extend your *if this* parts of code even further, as listed in Table 4-4. Figure 4-5, created using the file *logical_operators. php* from the companion archive, shows these operators being used in expressions.

Operator	Description	Example	Result
&&	And	1 == 1 && 2 == 2	TRUE
||	Or	1 == 1 || 2 == 3	TRUE
xor	Exclusive Or	1 == 1 xor 2 == 2	FALSE
!	Not	!(1 == 1)	FALSE

Table 4: The logical operators.

The && operator (known as the and operator) allows you to test for multiple conditions being TRUE, saving you from having to write multiple lines of code by combining them into a single expression. You can also use the and operator in the same way, like this:

```
if ($a == 4 &&  $b == 7) // Do this
if ($a == 5 and $b == 8) // Do that
```

In this example the statement following the if() (just a comment in this instance) will be executed only if $a has a value of 4 and also $b has a value of 7. Or you can test whether at least one value is TRUE using either the || or the or operator, like this:

```
if ($a == 4 || $b == 7) // Do this
if ($a == 5 or $b == 8) // Do that
```

Here if either $a has the value 4 or $b has the value 7 then the statement after the if() will be executed, so only one of the expressions needs to evaluate to TRUE.

Then there is the exclusive or operator, xor, which is TRUE if either part of the two halves of an expression is TRUE, or FALSE if they both are TRUE. To better understand this imagine you need to clean the kitchen floor and you have two containers of cleaning chemicals. One contains ammonia and one contains bleach. Now, as you know, it's dangerous to mix both these chemicals together as they produce a toxic gas, so we definitely don't want to use them both on the floor.

We can create an analogue of this using PHP code, like this:

```
$a = TRUE;        // Use Ammonia

$b = FALSE;       // Don't use Bleach


if ($a xor $b) // Is TRUE so clean the floor
```

What this code states is that if either $a is TRUE or $b is true then go ahead and clean the floor. But if both are FALSE the floor is not to be cleaned because no chemical has been selected. And if both are TRUE the floor also is not to be cleaned because it is dangerous to use both chemicals at once.

Lastly, you can negate any expression using the ! symbol (known as the not operator) by placing it in front of the expression (generally placing the expression within brackets too, so that the ! doesn't apply only to a part of the expression), like this:

```
if (!(++$lives > $max_lives)) // Carry on playing
```

In this example, if the variable $lives is incremented and its new value is not greater than the number of lives allowed (as stored in the value in $max_lives) the result of the expression is FALSE. Then the ! operator negates this to turn that value into TRUE. Therefore the statement after the if() will be executed since the player still has at least one life remaining.

On the other hand, if $lives increments to a value greater than $max_lives then the expression evaluates to TRUE, which is negated to FALSE, and so the code after the if() is not executed. Therefore the expression equates to the semi-English sentence "Use up a life, then if all lives have not yet been used execute the code supplied".

Note: When an expression can only return either a TRUE or FALSE value it is known as a Boolean expression. When combined with and, or and the not operator (&& and || and !) such expressions are said to use Boolean logic.

The Ternary Operator

Ever on the lookout for ways to make program code simpler and more compact, program language developers also came up with a thing called the ternary operator, which allows you to combine "If this then do that thing otherwise do another thing" type logic into a single expression, like this:

```
echo $lives > $max_lives ? 'Game over' : 'Keep playing';
```

The way the ternary operator works is that you provide an expression that can return either TRUE or FALSE (a Boolean expression). Following this you put a ? character, after which you place the two options, separated with a : character, as follows:

```
expression ? do this : do that;
```

For example, another ternary expression might go like the following, which sets the string variable $AmPm to either 'AM' or 'PM', according to the numeric value in the variable $Time:

```
$AmPm = $Time < 12 ? 'AM' : 'PM';
```

Bitwise Operators

There is a type of operator supported by PHP that as a beginner to programming you are most unlikely to use, due to it being quite advanced, and that's the bitwise operator. This type of operator acts on the individual 0 and 1 bits that make up binary numbers, and can be quite tricky to use.

The bitwise operators are &, |, ^, ~, <<, and >>. In order they support bitwise and, or, exclusive or, not, left-shift, and right-shift on binary numbers. The bitwise operators can also be combined with the = assignment operator to make a whole new collection of bitwise assignment operators.

However, this is a crash course on PHP and not an advanced tutorial so I shan't go into how you use them, because you already have enough new stuff to learn as it is. But for the curious who would like to know more about them, you can check out the following web page which covers them in some detail:

```
php.net/manual/en/language.operators.bitwise.php
```

Operator Precedence

In PHP some operators are given a higher precedence than others. For example, multiplication has a higher precedence than addition, so in the following expression the multiplication will occur *before* the addition, even though the addition appears first:

Precedence	Operators	Precedence	Operators
1	`clone new`	12	`&`
2	`() []`	13	`^`
3	`++ --`	14	`|`
4	`~ - (int) (float) (string) (array) (object) (bool) @`	15	`&&`
5	`instanceof`	16	`||`
6	`!`	17	`? :`
7	`* / %`	18	`= += -= *= /= .= %= &= |= ^= <<= >>= =>`
8	`+ - .`	19	`and`
9	`<< >>`	20	`xor`
10	`< <= > >= <>`	21	`or`
11	`== != === !==`	22	`,`

Table 5: Operator precedence - 1 is highest.

```
$MyVar = 3 + 4 * 5;
```

The result of this expression is 23 (4 * 5 is 20, 3 + 20 is 23). But if there were no operator precedence (with the expression executed simply from left to right) it would evaluate to 35 (3 + 4 is 7, 7 * 5 is 35).

By providing precedence to operators it obviates the need for parentheses, since the only way to make the preceding expression come out to 23 without operator precedence would be to insert parentheses as follows:

```
$MyVar = 3 + (4 * 5);
```

With this concept in mind, the creators of PHP have divided all the operators up into varying levels of precedence according to how 'important' they are (in that multiplication is considered more 'important' than addition due to its greater ability to create larger numbers). For the same reason division is given greater precedence than subtraction, and so on.

Therefore, unless you intend to use parentheses in all your expressions to ensure the correct precedence (which would make your code much harder to write, and for others to understand, due to multiple levels of parentheses), you need to know these precedencies, which are listed in Table 4-5:

All you need to learn from this table, though, is which operators have higher precedence than others, where 1 is the highest and 22 is the lowest precedence. So where an operator has lower precedence but you need to elevate it, all you need to do is apply parentheses in the right places for the operators within them to have raised precedence:

Operator Associativity

PHP operators also have an attribute known as associativity, which is the direction in which they should be evaluated. For example, the assignment operators all have right-to-left associativity because you are assigning the value on the right to the variable on the left, like this:

```
$MyVar = 0;
```

Because of this right-to-left associativity you can string assignments together, setting more than one variable at a time to a given value, like this:

```
$MyVar = $ThatVar = $OtherVar = 0;
```

This works because associativity of assignments starts at the right and continues in a leftward direction. In this instance $OtherVar is first assigned the value 0. Then $ThatVar is assigned the value in $OtherVar, and finally $MyVar is assigned the value in $ThatVar.

On the other hand, some operators have left-to-right associativity, such as the || (or) operator for example. You see, because of left-to-right associativity the process of executing PHP can be speeded up, as demonstrated in the following example:

```
if ($ThisVar == 1 || $ThatVar == 1) // Do this
```

Associativity	Operators
non-associative	`clone new ++ -- instanceof < <= > >= <> == != === !==`
right-to-left	`~ - (int) (float) (string) (array) (object) (bool) @` `! = += -= *= /= .= %= &= |= ^= <<= >>= =>`
left-to-right	`() [] * / % + - . << >> & ^	&& || ?: and xor or ,`

Table 6: Operator associativity.

When PHP encounters the `||` operator it knows to check the left-hand side first. So, if `$ThisVar` has a value of `1` there is no need to look up the value of `$ThatVar`, because as long as one or the other expression either side of the `||` operator evaluates to TRUE, the `||` expression evaluates to TRUE, and if the left half has evaluated to TRUE, so has the whole `||` expression. In cases such as this, the PHP interpreter will eagerly skip the second half of the expression, knowing it is running in an optimized fashion.

Knowing whether operators have right-to-left or left-to-right associativity can really help your programming. For example, if you are using a left-to-right associative operator such as `||` you can line up all your expressions left to right from the most to the least important.

Therefore it's worth taking a moment to familiarize yourself with the contents of Table 4-6, so that you will know which operators have what associativity.

Summary

This lecture has brought you up to scratch with all you need to know about using operators, so now you're ready to start looking at some of PHP's more complex and interesting objects in the following lecture on arrays.

PHP
ARRAYS

By following this lecture you will:

- ✓ *Be able to use numeric and string arrays for storing values.*
- ✓ *Understand how to add and retrieve array data.*
- ✓ *Know how to handle associative arrays.*

PHP IS CAPABLE of managing data in a more powerful manner than simply via variables. One example of this is PHP arrays, which you can think of as collections of variables grouped together. For example, a good metaphor for an array might be a filing cabinet with each drawer representing a different variable, as shown in Figure 5-1.

As with the small pot metaphor in Lecture 3, with the filing cabinet to assign a value you should imagine writing it down on pieces of paper, placing it in the relevant drawer and closing it. To read back a value you open the drawer, take out the paper, read its value, return the paper and close the drawer. The only difference between the cabinet and the pots is that the drawers of the filing cabinet (representing an array) are all in sequential order, whereas a collection of pots (representing variables) are stored in no particular order.

Although PHP arrays can be any size (up to the available memory in your computer), for the sake of simplicity I have only shown ten elements in the figure. You can access each of the elements in an array numerically, starting with element 0 (the top drawer of the cabinet). This index number is important, because you might think that logically the number 1 would be the best starting point, but that isn't how PHP arrays are accessed – you should always remember that the first element is the zeroth.

Figure 1: A filing cabinet representing a 10-element array.

Array Names

The rules for naming arrays are exactly the same as those for naming variables. Array names must begin with a $ symbol. Followed by either an upper or lower case letter (a-z or A-Z), or the _ symbol. No other character may begin an array name.

Array names may not contain any mathematical operators (such as + or *), punctuation (such as ! or &), or spaces, but after the first character they may include the digits 0-9 or any upper or lower case letters (a-z or A-Z), or the _ symbol.

Creating an Array

To create an array you can declare it in advance to initialize it, like this:

```
$MyArray = array()
```

This array object contains no data but is ready for data to be assigned to its elements.

Assigning Values to an Array Element

You can populate arrays with data (in a similar manner to assigning values to variables) like this:

```
$MyArray[0] = 23;
$MyArray[1] = 67.35;
```

Here the integer 23 is assigned to element 0 (the top drawer of the cabinet), while the floating point number 67.35 is assigned to the index at element 1 (the second drawer down – because they begin at 0). In fact you can assign any legal value to an array element, including strings, objects, and even other arrays (which I'll come to in Lecture 5), like this:

```
$MyArray[3] = "Hello world";
$MyArray[4] = $OtherArray;
```

You are not restricted to assigning values in order, so you can go right in and assign values to any elements, like this:

```
$MyArray[9] = "Good morning";
$MyArray[7] = 3.1415927;
```

If you don't need your data stored in any particular array elements you can, instead, insert values into the next available element of an array by omitting the element number. Therefore the previous six assignments could be made like this:

```
$MyArray[] = 23;
$MyArray[] = 67.35;
$MyArray[] = "Hello world";
$MyArray[] = $OtherArray;
$MyArray[] = "Good morning";
$MyArray[] = 3.1415927;
```

Using Indexes

The element number we have been using for storing a particular value is known as the array *index*, and you can use integer (as shown so far) or variable values as indexes. For example, the following first creates a variable and assigns it a numeric value, which is then used to assign another value to the array:

```
$MyIndex          = 123;
$MyArray[$MyIndex] = "Good evening";
```

This has the effect of assigning the string value "Good evening" to the element with an index of 123 in $MyArray[].

Retrieving Values

Once an array has been created and it has been populated with data, to retrieve a value from an array you simply refer to it, like this:

```
echo $MyArray[0];
```

This will fetch the value stored in the zeroth element of $MyArray[] (or the top drawer of the filing cabinet metaphor) and then pass it to echo to display it in the browser. You can, likewise, return a value using a variable, like this:

```
$MyIndex = 713;
echo $MyArray[$MyIndex];
```

Whatever value is stored in element 713 of the array will then be displayed in the browser.

Note: The preceding two examples (and many following ones) assume you have already created an array.

There are other ways you can use array values, such as assigning them to other variables or other array elements, or using them in expressions. For example, the following code assigns the value 23 to an array element, which is then looked up and used in an expression, in which 50 is added to it and the result (73) is displayed in the browser:

Figure 2: Displaying a value in an alert window.

```
$MyArray[7] = 23;
echo $MyArray[7] + 50;
```

Or, for example, you may wish to display a value in an JavaScript alert window using code such as the following, which results in your browser looking like Figure 5-2 (although the style of the window varies by browser):

```
$MyArray[7] = 23;
echo '<script>alert(' . $MyArray[7] + 50 . ')</script>';
```

Using Array Elements as Indexes

You can even go a step further and use the value stored in an array element as an index into another (or the same) array, like this:

```
$OtherArray[0]            = 77;
$MyArray[$OtherArray[0]] = "I love the movie Inception";
```

Here the zeroth element of $OtherArray[] is assigned the integer value of 77. Once assigned, this element is used as the index into $MyArray[] (rather like the movie *Inception*, with arrays within arrays). However, this is quite complex programming and you are unlikely to use these types of indexes as a beginner to PHP.

Note: The fact that you can use any valid integer value (including values in variables, array elements and those returned by functions) means that you can use mathematical equations to iterate through arrays. For example, as you will discover in Lecture 8, it is easy to create code that runs in a loop to process each element of an array in turn.

Other Ways of Creating Arrays

You have already seen the following type of declaration for creating a PHP array:

```
$MyArray = array();
```

But there are also a couple of other methods you can use, which also have the effect of simplifying your code, by allowing you to populate the array with some data at the same time. The first method is as follows:

```
$MyArray = array(123, "Hello there", 3.21);
```

Here the array `$MyArray[]` is created and its first three elements immediately populated with three different values: an integer, a string and a floating point number. This is equivalent to the following (much longer) code:

```
$MyArray      = array();
$MyArray[0] = 123;
$MyArray[1] = "Hello there";
$MyArray[2] = 3.21;
```

Note: Once you have created an array, if you need to apply any more values to elements within it, you must use the standard form of assigning values. If you re-use the short form of combined array creation and value assignment, it will simply reset the array to the values in the assignment.

Using Associative Arrays

Using numeric indexes is all well and good when you only have a few elements in an array to cope with. But once an array starts to hold meaningful amounts of data, using numbers to access its elements can be highly confusing. Thankfully PHP provides a great solution to this by supporting the use of names to associate with array elements, in much the same way that variables have names.

Let's use PHP's associative arrays to store the ages of the players in a mixed, under eleven, five-a-side soccer team. Here the array is initialized and then the age of each player is assigned to an element in the array using the player's names:

```
$SoccerTeam = array();
$SoccerTeam['Andy']  = 10;
$SoccerTeam['Brian'] = 8;
$SoccerTeam['Cathy'] = 9;
$SoccerTeam['David'] = 10;
$SoccerTeam['Ellen'] = 9;
```

Having been assigned, these values they can now easily be looked up by name, like this, which displays Cathy's age in the browser:

```
echo SoccerTeam['Cathy'];
```

Keys, Values, and Hash Tables

When you use associative arrays you are actually creating a collection of *key* and *value* pairs. The name you assign to an array element is known as the key, while the value you provide to the element is the value.

In other languages (such as JavaScript) this type of data structure is known as a *hash table*. When an object (such as a string) is used as a key for a value this is called a hash value, and the data structure is a hash table.

Other Ways of Creating an Associative Array

If you wish, you can use a short from of creating and populating an associative array, like this:

```
$SoccerTeam = array(
   'Andy'  => 10,
   'Brian' => 8,
```

```
        'Cathy'  => 9,
        'David'  => 10,
        'Ellen'  => 9
    );
```

I'm sure you'll agree this is much simpler and easier to use, once you know that this type of code structure causes the creation of an array. But you may prefer to stick with the longer form until you are completely happy with using arrays. Also, I have chosen to be liberal with newlines here for reasons of clarity, but if you wish you can run all these five sub-statements into a single line.

As with standard variables and arrays, you are not restricted to only storing numbers in associative arrays, because you can assign any valid value, including integers, floating point numbers, strings, and even other arrays and objects. The following illustrates a couple of these:

```
    $MyInfo = array(
        'Name'        => 'Bill Gates',
        'Age'         => 56,
        'Occupation' => 'Philanthropist',
        'Children'    => 3,
        'Worth'       => 59000000000
    );
```

In the preceding example both strings and numbers have been assigned to the array elements. You can read back any value simply by referring to it, like this, which displays the value in 'Occupation' (namely 'Philanthropist') in the browser:

```
    echo $MyInfo['Occupation'];
```

Summary

By now you'll have a pretty good understanding of PHP arrays and will be beginning to see how they can make excellent structures for handling your data. In the following lecture I'll show you how there's actually a lot more to arrays than you've so far seen, and we'll begin to make some reasonably complex data objects.

MULTI-DIMENSIONAL ARRAYS

By following this lecture you will:

- ✓ *Be able to use more than one level of nested arrays.*
- ✓ *Know how to create associative multidimensional arrays.*
- ✓ *Be familiar with populating large arrays with data.*

LET ME START by totally contradicting the title of this lecture and stating that there's actually no such thing as multidimensional arrays in PHP. But before you start scratching your head and wondering whether I've drunk too many cups of tea, let me say that you can *simulate* multidimensional arrays in PHP by assigning new arrays as the values for elements of an existing array.

But what exactly do I mean by *multidimensional* in the first place? Well, in the same way that a string of characters is a collection of individual letters, numbers and other characters, that you can imagine being like a string of pearls – with each pearl occupying its right location, and the correct pearls on either side, all in the right order, an array, therefore, is like a collection of variables all stored in their right locations.

In the previous lecture I used the metaphor of a filing cabinet for an array of ten elements. If you imagine for a moment that each drawer in this filing cabinet is like *Doctor Who*'s Tardis (his time and space machine) in that it is much bigger on the inside than it is on the outside, then you should be able to also imagine being able to place another ten-drawer filing cabinet in each of the drawers of the original one! Figure 6-1 should help make this clearer.

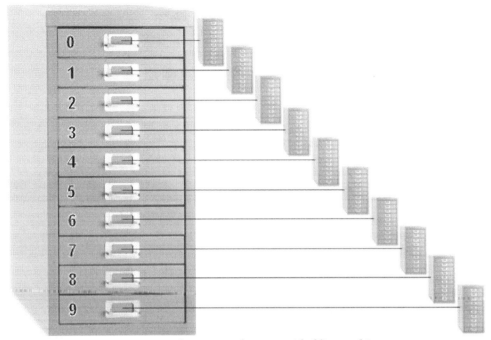

Figure 1: Representing a two-dimensional array with filing cabinets.

Remember that these particular filing cabinets are not bound by the normal rules of space and time, so that the small cabinets can contain just as much as the large one.

In fact the cabinets are capable of holding an infinite amount of data, limited only by the restraints of your browser, operating system and available memory. I have simply drawn the secondary filing cabinets much smaller so that they fit into the figure.

Creating a Two-Dimensional Array

Let's see how we can use the ability of an array element being able to store another entire array to our advantage by considering a ten times multiplication table, just like those often found on the walls of school children (see Figure 6-2).

Each of the columns (or each of the rows) can be considered a one-dimensional array. For example, the first row could be created using the following code:

	1	2	3	4	5	6	7	8	9	10
1	1	2	3	4	5	6	7	8	9	10
2	2	4	6	8	10	12	14	16	18	20
3	3	6	9	12	15	18	21	24	27	30
4	4	8	12	16	20	24	28	32	36	40
5	5	10	15	20	25	30	35	40	45	50
6	6	12	18	24	30	36	42	48	54	60
7	7	14	21	28	35	42	49	56	63	70
8	8	16	24	32	40	48	56	64	72	80
9	9	18	27	36	45	54	63	72	81	90
10	10	20	40	40	50	60	70	80	90	100

Figure 2: A ten times multiplication table.

```
$MyTable0     = array();
$MyTable0[0] = 1;
$MyTable1[1] = 2;
$MyTable2[2] = 3;
$MyTable3[3] = 4;
$MyTable4[4] = 5;
$MyTable5[5] = 6;
$MyTable6[6] = 7;
$MyTable7[7] = 8;
$MyTable8[8] = 9;
$MyTable9[9] = 10;
```

Or, more succinctly:

```
$MyTable0 = array(1, 2, 3, 4, 5, 6, 7, 8, 9, 10);
```

Similarly, the second row could be created like this:

```
$MyTable1 = array(2, 4, 6, 8, 10, 12, 14, 16, 18, 20);
```

And so you can go on for rows three through ten, so that you end up with the following set of statements:

```
$MyTable0 = array( 1,  2,  3,  4,  5,  6,  7,  8,  9, 10);
$MyTable1 = array( 2,  4,  6,  8, 10, 12, 14, 16, 18, 20);
$MyTable2 = array( 3,  6,  9, 12, 15, 18, 21, 24, 27, 20);
$MyTable3 = array( 4,  8, 12, 16, 20, 24, 28, 32, 36, 20);
$MyTable4 = array( 5, 10, 15, 20, 25, 30, 35, 40, 45, 20);
$MyTable5 = array( 6, 12, 18, 24, 30, 36, 42, 48, 54, 20);
$MyTable6 = array( 7, 14, 21, 28, 35, 42, 49, 56, 63, 20);
$MyTable7 = array( 8, 16, 24, 32, 40, 48, 56, 64, 72, 20);
$MyTable8 = array( 9, 18, 27, 36, 45, 54, 63, 72, 81, 20);
$MyTable9 = array(10, 20, 30, 40, 50, 60, 70, 80, 90,100);
```

At this point we now have 10 arrays – one for each row in the times table. With these now created, it is now possible to build a two-dimensional table by creating just one more, master, table, like this:

```
$MasterTable    = array();
$MasterTable[0] = $MyTable0;
$MasterTable[1] = $MyTable1;
$MasterTable[2] = $MyTable2;
$MasterTable[3] = $MyTable3;
$MasterTable[4] = $MyTable4;
$MasterTable[5] = $MyTable5;
$MasterTable[6] = $MyTable6;
$MasterTable[7] = $MyTable7;
$MasterTable[8] = $MyTable8;
$MasterTable[9] = $MyTable9;
```

Or by using the shorter form of:

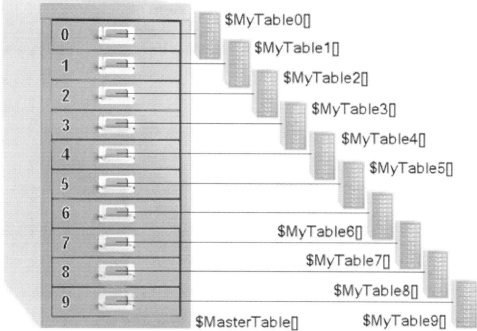

Figure 3: The relationship between the cabinets and arrays.

```
$MasterTable = array
(
    $MyTable0,
    $MyTable1,
    $MyTable2,
    $MyTable3,
    $MyTable4,
    $MyTable5,
    $MyTable6,
    $MyTable7,
    $MyTable8,
    $MyTable9
);
```

Note: I have chosen to split this up into multiple lines for clarity, but you can equally include all the preceding in a single statement on one line.

Accessing a Two-Dimensional Array

Let's now look at how this relates to the filing cabinets in Figure 6-1 in terms of code. To recap, there's a main array called `$MasterTable[]`, and its ten elements each contain another array named `$MyTable0[]` through `$MyTable9[]`.

As you will recall from the previous lecture, accessing an array is as simple as the following, which displays the value in the array held at a numeric index of 23 (which will be element 24 since arrays start from 0) in an alert window:

```
echo $SomeArray[23];
```

But what should you do when the value stored in an array element is another array? The answer is simple and elegant – you simply add another pair of square brackets following the first pair, and place an index value into that new array between them, like this:

```
echo $MasterTable[0][0];
```

This statement displays the contents of the first element of the array that is stored in the first element of `$MasterTable[]`. Notice that there is no need to reference the sub-array (sub-array being the term I use for referring to arrays within arrays) by name.

Likewise, if you wish to display the value held in the seventh row of the array stored in the third element of `$MasterTable[]` you would use code such as this (remembering that table indexes start at 0 not 1, so the seventh and third elements will be 6 and 2 respectively):

```
echo $MasterTable[2][6];
```

In terms of the times table in Figure 6-2 this is equivalent to first moving to the seventh column along, and then down to the third row, at which point you can see that the value shown is 21, as you will quickly see if you look at the source of *timestable.htm* (available in the companion archive):

```
<!DOCTYPE html>
<html>
  <head>
    <title>Two-Dimensional Array Example</title>
  </head>
  <body>
<?php
    $MyTable0 = array( 1,  2,  3,  4,  5,  6,  7,  8,  9, 10);
    $MyTable1 = array( 2,  4,  6,  8, 10, 12, 14, 16, 18, 20);
    $MyTable2 = array( 3,  6,  9, 12, 15, 18, 21, 24, 27, 20);
    $MyTable3 = array( 4,  8, 12, 16, 20, 24, 28, 32, 36, 20);
    $MyTable4 = array( 5, 10, 15, 20, 25, 30, 35, 40, 45, 20);
    $MyTable5 = array( 6, 12, 18, 24, 30, 36, 42, 48, 54, 20);
    $MyTable6 = array( 7, 14, 21, 28, 35, 42, 49, 56, 63, 20);
    $MyTable7 = array( 8, 16, 24, 32, 40, 48, 56, 64, 72, 20);
    $MyTable8 = array( 9, 18, 27, 36, 45, 54, 63, 72, 81, 20);
    $MyTable9 = array(10, 20, 30, 40, 50, 60, 70, 80, 90,100);


    $MasterTable = array($MyTable0, $MyTable1, $MyTable2,
                         $MyTable3, $MyTable4, $MyTable5,
                         $MyTable6, $MyTable7, $MyTable8,
                         $MyTable9);


    echo 'The value at location 2,6 is ' . $MasterTable[2][6];
?>
  </body>
</html>
```

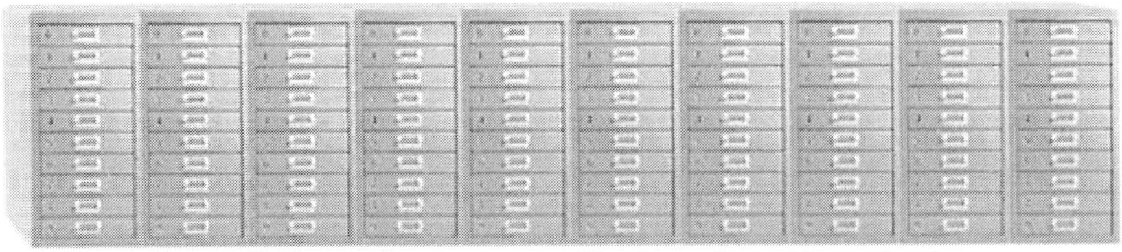

Figure 4: The small filing cabinets are now lined up alongside each other.

Note: *This code is equivalent to the filing cabinets in Figure 6-1, in that the $MasterTable[] array represents the large cabinet, while the $myTable0[] array is the top small cabinet, and $myTable9[] is the bottom small cabinet, as shown in Figure 6-3.*

If you now take all the small filing cabinets and stack them up alongside each other, you will now see how they represent the $MasterTable[] array, as shown in Figure 6-4. To all intents and purposes we can forget about the main array (other than for using its name to index into the sub-arrays), and think only terms of the ten sub-arrays, and how to access each drawer using pairs of indexes.

The first index goes along the drawers of cabinets from left to right, and the second one goes down the drawers top to bottom. Therefore array index [3][7] points to the fourth filing cabinet along and the eighth drawer down.

In other words, $MasterTable[3][7] refers to the value held in the eighth drawer down of the fourth cabinet along.

A More Practical Example

Obviously a multiplication table is a trivial thing to recreate on a computer, as it can be achieved with a couple of simple loops. So let's look instead at a more practical example: that of a board for a game of chess.

As you will know, there are 64 squares on a chess board, laid out in an 8 × 8 grid, and there are two sets of 16 pieces: black and white. Using a computer to represent a chess board in its starting position, and ignoring the fact that the squares alternate between dark and light, you might use code such as this (in which upper case letters represent white pieces, and the lower case ones are black):

```
$Row0 = array('r', 'n', 'b', 'q', 'k', 'b', 'n', 'r');

$Row1 = array('p', 'p', 'p', 'p', 'p', 'p', 'p', 'p');

$Row2 = array('-', '-', '-', '-', '-', '-', '-', '-');

$Row3 = array('-', '-', '-', '-', '-', '-', '-', '-');

$Row4 = array('-', '-', '-', '-', '-', '-', '-', '-');

$Row5 = array('-', '-', '-', '-', '-', '-', '-', '-');

$Row6 = array('P', 'P', 'P', 'P', 'P', 'P', 'P', 'P');

$Row7 = array('R', 'N', 'B', 'Q', 'K', 'B', 'N', 'R');
```

The dashes represent locations where there is no chess piece, and the key for the other letters is as follows:

- **R/r** Rooks
- **N/n** Knights
- **B/b** Bishops
- **Q/q** Queens
- **K/k** Kings
- **P/p** Pawns

You can now insert all these arrays into a master array that holds the complete chess board, like this:

```
$Board = array($Row0, $Row1, $Row2, $Row3,
               $Row4, $Row5, $Row6, $Row7);
```

Now we are ready to move pieces about on the board. So, for example, let's assume that the white player opens with the standard *pawn to king 4* move. Using the array notation of locations [0][0] through [7][7], with [0][0] being the top left corner, and [7][7] the bottom right, this is equivalent to setting the location [6][4] to '-' to remove the pawn currently at this location, and then setting [4][4] to 'P' to place the pawn in its new position. In terms of code it would look like this:

```
$Temp        = $Board[6][4];

$Board[6][4] = '-';

$Board[4][4] = Temp;
```

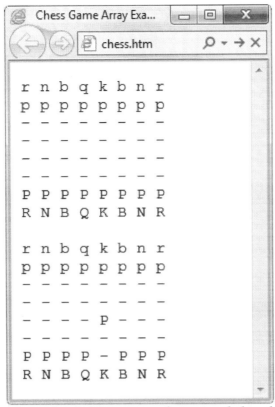

Figure 5: Modifying a two-dimensional chess board array.

In this example a new variable called `Temp` is employed to store the value extracted from `$Board[6][4]`. Then `$Board[6][4]` is set to a dash character to remove the piece, and the value now in `Temp` is then placed into `$Board[4][4]`, overwriting whatever value it previously held.

Or, if it's not necessary to hold a copy of the piece being moved (which it isn't in this very simple simulation), then you can simply set the two array locations to their required values, like this:

```
$Board[6][4] = '-';
$Board[4][4] = 'P';
```

Figure 6-5 shows the *chess.php* example file (available in the companion archive), in which the before and after board positions are shown, as created by the preceding code.

Note: If you wish you may continue adding arrays within other arrays until you run out of computer memory. All you do is place new arrays inside existing ones to add an extra dimension. For example, If you were to create an additional 8 sub-sub-arrays for each of the sub-array elements (a total of 64 new arrays), you would form eight complete chessboards in a three-dimensional array, representing an 8 × 8 × 8 cube!

Multidimensional Associative Arrays

As you might expect, as with numeric arrays, you can create multidimensional associative arrays. Let me explain why you might want to do this by considering a small on-line store that sells toys for six different age ranges of children, as follows

- Babies
- Toddlers
- Age 3-5
- Age 5-8
- Age 8-12
- Teenagers

These categories can be easily mapped into an associative array, as I'll show you in a minute. But let's first create some sub-categories for each of the main ones, such as these:

- Babies
    - Rattle
    - Bear
    - Pacifier
- Toddlers
    - Wooden Bricks
    - Xylophone
    - Play Dough
- Age 3-5
    - Slide
    - Tricycle
    - Crayons
- Age 5-8
    - Dolly
    - Bicycle
    - Guitar
- Age 8-12
    - Tablet Computer
    - Remote Control Car

- o Frisbee
- Teenagers
  - o MP3 Player
  - o Game Console
  - o TV/DVD Combo

Clearly these sub-categories can also be mapped to associative arrays, but before we do that we have to go even deeper (yet more undertones of *Inception*) because a web store needs things like pricing information and product availability, like this:

- Price
- Stock Level

Creating the Multi-Dimensional Array

Armed with these details we're now ready to start building the arrays needed, by assigning values to the price and stock level of each product being sold to a two-dimensional array for each product, as follows:

```
$Rattle    = array('Price' =>    4.99, 'Stock' => 3 );

$Bear      = array('Price' =>    6.99, 'Stock' => 2 );

$Pacifier  = array('Price' =>    1.99, 'Stock' => 9 );

$Bricks    = array('Price' =>    5.99, 'Stock' => 1 );

$Xylophone = array('Price' =>   12.99, 'Stock' => 2 );

$PlayDough = array('Price' =>    8.49, 'Stock' => 7 );

$Slide     = array('Price' =>   99.99, 'Stock' => 1 );

$Tricycle  = array('Price' =>   79.99, 'Stock' => 1 );

$Crayons   = array('Price' =>    3.79, 'Stock' => 5 );

$Dolly     = array('Price' =>   14.99, 'Stock' => 3 );

$Bicycle   = array('Price' =>   89.99, 'Stock' => 2 );

$Guitar    = array('Price' =>   49.00, 'Stock' => 1 );

$TabletPC  = array('Price' => 149.99, 'Stock' => 1 );

$RemoteCar = array('Price' =>   39.99, 'Stock' => 2 );

$Frisbee   = array('Price' =>    7.99, 'Stock' => 6 );

$MP3Player = array('Price' => 179.99, 'Stock' => 1 );
```

```
$Console    = array('Price' => 199.99, 'Stock' => 2 );
$TVAndDVD   = array('Price' =>  99.99, 'Stock' => 1 );
```

Now that these basic data structures are complete it's possible to group the products into the age range arrays, like this (where the words in quotes are the keys and those after the => operators are the values, which are the names of the arrays previously created):

```
$Babies    = array('Rattle'            => $Rattle,
                   'Bear'              => $Bear,
                   'Pacifier'          => $Pacifier);
$Toddlers  = array('Wooden Bricks'     => $Bricks,
                   'Xylophone'         => $Xylophone,
                   'Play Dough'        => $PlayDough);
$Age3_5    = array('Slide'             => $Slide,
                   'Tricycle'          => $Tricycle,
                   'Crayons'           => $Crayons);
$Age5_8    = array('Dolly'             => $Dolly,
                   'Bicycle'           => $Bicycle,
                   'Guitar'            => $Guitar);
$Age8_12   = array('Tablet PC'         => $TabletPC,
                   'Remote Control Car' => $RemoteCar,
                   'Frisbee'           => $Frisbee);
$Teenagers = array('MP3 Player'        => $MP3Player,
                   'Game Console'      => $Console,
                   'TV/DVD Combo'      => $TVAndDVD);
```

Note: I used an underline character between the digits in these age rage arrays since the dash is a disallowed character in variable or array names (because it can be confused with the minus symbol). The dash is acceptable, however, when used as part of a quoted string for a key name.

And finally the top array can be populated, like this (where the strings in quotes are the keys, and the values after the => operators are the names of the arrays just defined):

```
$Categories= array('Toddlers'  => $Toddlers,
                    'Ages 3-5'  => $Age3_5,
                    'Ages 5-8'  => $Age5_8,
                    'Ages 8-12' => $Age8_12,
                    'Teenagers' => $Teenagers);
```

What has now been created is actually a three-dimensional array. The first dimension is the $Categories[] array, the second is each of the age range arrays, and the third is each of the product arrays containing the price and stock level.

Note: Remember that in each of these assignments the string on the left is the key and the item on the right is the value. In all but the innermost (or lowest) case the value is the name of another array that has already been created. For the innermost case the values are numeric values: the price and stock level.

Accessing the Arrays

You can now read and write to these stored values in the following manner, which returns the price of the slide, which is 99.99 (no currency type is specified in these examples, just values):

```
echo $Categories['Ages 3-5']['Slide']['Price'];
```

Or, if you need to change a price on an item of inventory for any reason, such as the crayons for example (currently 3.79), you can alter it in the following manner, which reduces the price by 0.20:

```
$Categories['Ages 3-5']['Crayons']['Price'] = 3.59;
```

Likewise, when you sell an item of stock you can reduce the inventory level (the stock level) in a similar manner, such as the following which decreases the stock level of game consoles by 1 using the pre-decrement operator:

```
--$Categories['Teenagers']['Game Console']['Stock'];
```

Obviously the inventory for even the smallest on-line store is sure to be far greater than in this example, and there are going to be many additional attributes for some toys, such as different sizes and colors and even any images, descriptions, technical specifications or other details about the product that are available, all of which could easily be built into this multi-dimensional structure of arrays.

The file *toystore.php* in the companion archive contains all the preceding pre-populated arrays and the example statements that access them. You may wish to try experimenting with it to read from and write to other items of data within the array structure.

Summary

You should be starting to see why I called this a crash course because we've now covered a huge amount of territory in just 6 lectures. Hopefully, though, it's all making sense to you, and arrays are beginning to feel like second nature. Therefore, in the next lecture we'll look at some fun we can have using the array accessing functions provided with PHP.

THE PHP ARRAY FUNCTIONS

By studying the contents this lecture you will:

- ✓ *Learn all the most useful array handling functions.*
- ✓ *Be able to join and split arrays to and from each other.*
- ✓ *Know how to sort arrays in various ways.*

TO MAKE ARRAYS even more powerful, PHP comes ready-made with a selection of handy functions for accessing and manipulating arrays. For example you can join arrays together, push new items into an array (and pop them off again later), reverse the data in an array, sort it alphabetically or numerically, and more.

So, in this lecture, we'll look at a small selection of these functions and how to use them. If you would like to see the complete set of array functions, you can view the documentation page at:

```
php.net/manual/en/ref.array.php
```

Using `foreach()`

The first feature I'd like to introduce is `foreach()`, because with it you can iterate through an array one element at a time, which we will need to do in the following examples in order to see the results. To show how this iteration works let's start with a simple array:

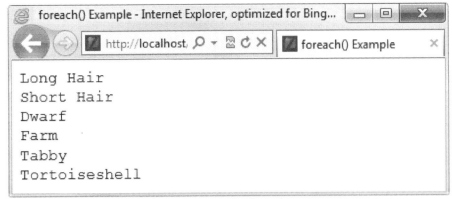

Figure 1: The contents of $Cats() is displayed.

```
$Cats = array('Long Hair', 'Short Hair', 'Dwarf',
              'Farm',       'Tabby',       'Tortoiseshell');
```

Now, let's use `foreach` to display all its elements, as follows (resulting in Figure 7-1):

```
foreach($Cats as $cat)
{
   echo "$cat<br />";
}
```

What's happening here is the `as` keyword creates a new variable called $cat, which takes on the value in each element of $Cats[] in turn, as the loop iterates through the array. Then the contents of the curly braces is executed once for each element in the $Cats[] until there are no more elements left in the array to process.

Note: Here you see one of my programming styles, which is to use the plural of a word for an array name, and the singular for a single element in that array (as extracted by `foreach()` *for example). I also choose to make the singular variable all lower case to further indicate that it is only a member of a larger object.*

For reasons I will explain in Lecture 11 the curly braces can be omitted when there is only a single statement to be executed by such a loop. Therefore, for the sake of simplicity in the following examples, I will reduce this type of code to the much shorter following example:

```
foreach($Cats as $cat) echo "$cat<br />";
```

In an associative array you can also use `foreach()` to extract both the key and the value for each element. For example, consider the soccer team array from Lecture 5:

```
$SoccerTeam = array(
   'Andy'  => 10,
   'Brian' => 8,
   'Cathy' => 9,
   'David' => 10,
   'Ellen' => 9
);
```

Using `foreach()` you can extract all this data as follows:

```
foreach($SoccerTeam as $player => $age)
   echo "$player is $age years old<br />";
```

In this example, each time around the loop `$player` is given the key for the current element, and `$age` is set to the value for that element. Now that there's an easy way to display the contents of an array, we can start to look at the array functions provided by PHP, and see how to use them. You can try both of these examples for yourself by loading the *foreach.php* example from the companion archive into your browser.

Using `array_merge()`

Using the `array_merge()` function you can return a new array created by joining two other arrays together. The two original arrays are not changed in any way by this function, only the result of joining them together is returned.

To see how this works let's create a second array to go with the `$Cats[]` array created a little earlier, as follows:

```
$Dogs = array('Pit Bull', 'Spaniel',  'Terrier',
              'Beagle',   'Shepherd', 'Bulldog');
```

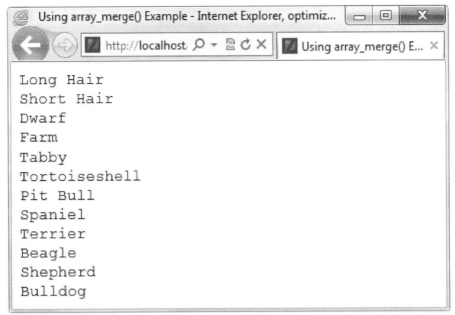

Figure 2: The two arrays have been merged.

With both arrays now created we can now run the `array_merge()` function on them, like this:

```
$Pets = array_merge($Cats, $Dogs);
```

And now to see the result of this operation we can issue the following statement:

```
foreach($Pets as $pet) echo "$pet<br />";
```

The code to create these two arrays and the preceding pair of statements are in the *array_merge.php* file in the companion archive.

As you can see in Figure 7-2 the result is that the new array `$Pets[]` now contains all elements from both the `$Cats[]` and `$Dogs[]` arrays, in order.

For a similar result, but with the contents of the `$Dogs[]` array before the `$Cats[]`, you could equally have issued this statement:

```
$Pets = array_merge($Dogs, $Cats);
```

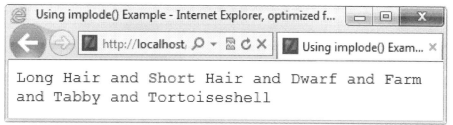

Figure 3: The result of imploding array elements into a string.

In fact, you could omit the creation of the `$Pets[]` array altogether and simply iterate through the result of the `array_merge()` call, like this:

```
foreach(array_merge($Cats, $Dogs) as $pet)
  echo "$pet<br />";
```

Using `implode()`

Sometimes you may wish to turn all the elements in an array into a string, and this is easy to do using the `implode()` function. For example, let's take the case of the `$Cats[]` array, as follows:

```
echo implode(' and ', $Cats);
```

This statement calls the `implode()` function, passing it the string `' and '`, which is used as a separator, which is inserted between each element, as shown in Figure 7-3. You may use any string as the element separator, or none at all, as in the following three examples:

```
echo implode($Cats);
echo implode('',  $Cats);
echo implode(',', $Cats);
```

When nothing or an empty string (`''`) is passed to `implode()` as its first argument, no separator is inserted between element values, while a comma or any other value passed to it is used as the separator. So, in turn, the three previous statements display the following:

```
Long HairShort HairDwarfFarmTabbyTortoiseshell
Long HairShort HairDwarfFarmTabbyTortoiseshell
Long Hair, Short Hair,Dwarf,Farm,Tabby,Tortoiseshell
```

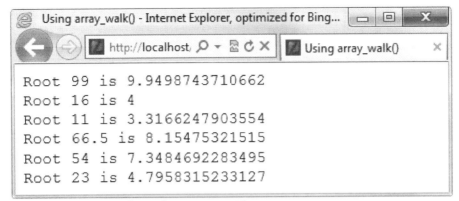

Figure 4: Iterating through an array with `array_walk()`.

Note: PHP also supports the alias (a copy of a function using a different name) of `join()`, *which works in an identical manner to* `implode()`.

The `array_walk()` Function

One very quick and easy way to process all the elements in an array is to pass the array to a function, via PHP's `array_walk()` function. For example, the following code creates an array populated with numbers, and then applies the new function `CalcRoot()` function to each element, all via a single call to the `array_walk()` function.

```
$Nums = array(99, 16, 11, 66.5, 54, 23);
array_walk($Nums, 'sqrt');


function CalcRoot($item)
{
    echo "Root $item is " . sqrt($item) . '<br />';
}
```

You can see the result of running this code (*array_walk.php* in the companion archive) in Figure 7-4.

Note: How to create and use your own functions (such as `CalcRoot()` *in this example) is fully detailed in Lecture 10.*

Using `array_push()`

There are a couple of good reasons for using the `array_push()` function. Firstly you can add a new element to the end of an array without knowing how many items already exist in that array. For example, normally you would need to know the current array length and then use that value to add extra values, like this (using the `$Cats[]` array once more):

```
$Cats        = array('Long Hair', 'Short Hair', 'Dwarf',
                      'Farm',       'Tabby',       'Tortoiseshell');
$len         = sizeof($Cats);
$Cats[$len] = 'Siamese';
```

The new variable `$len` is used to hold the length of the array (the number of elements it contains). In this instance the value will be 6, for elements 0 through 5. Therefore the value in `$len`, being 6, is suitable to use as an index into the next available element, and so that is what it is used for – the value 6 pointing to the seventh element, since element indexes start at 0.

In fact, if the variable `$len` is not to be used anywhere else it's actually superfluous, so you could replace the final two lines of the preceding example with this single statement:

```
$Cats[sizeof($Cats)] = 'Siamese';
```

However, it is much simpler to let PHP keep track of array lengths and simply tell it to add a new element to the `$Cats[]` array, like this:

```
array_push($Cats, 'Siamese');
```

You can verify that the element has been added with the following `foreach()` loop (which results in Figure 7-5, the code for which is available as *array_push.htm* in the companion archive):

```
foreach($Cats as $cat) echo "$cat<br />";
```

The second reason you might want to use `array_push()` is because it's a quick way of storing values in a sequence that then have to be recalled in the reverse order. For example, using `array_push()` you can keep adding elements to an array, like this:

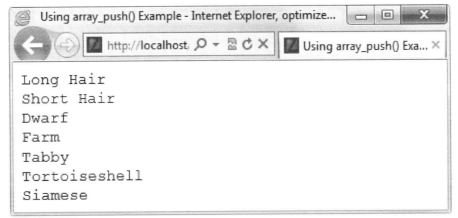

Figure 5: Pushing a new element onto an array.

```
array_push($MyArray, 'A');
array_push($MyArray, 'B');
array_push($MyArray, 'C');
```

Then, as you will see in the following description of array_pop(), you can also remove these elements from last to first, such that the value 'C' will be taken of first, then 'B', then 'A', and so on.

Using array_pop()

At its simplest array_pop() enables you to remove the last element from an array (and in this instance discard the returned value), using code such as this:

```
array_pop($MyArray);
```

Or, to remove the last element from an array and store it in a variable (for example), you use code such as this:

```
$MyVariable = array_pop($MyArray);
```

You can apply array_pop() to an existing array with values in, which can have been assigned when the array was created, via a call to array_push() or in any other way.

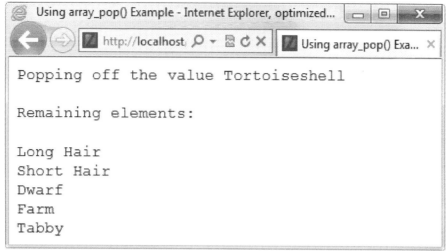

Figure 6: Popping an element off an array.

The `array_pop()` function then pulls the last item off the array (removing it from the array) and then returns that value. Looking again at the `$Cats[]` array, a working example might look like this:

```
$Cats = array('Long Hair', 'Short Hair', 'Dwarf',
              'Farm',       'Tabby',       'Tortoiseshell');

echo 'Popping off the value ' . array_pop($Cats) . '<br /><br />';
echo 'Remaining elements: <br /><br />';

foreach($Cats as $cat) echo "$cat<br />";
```

The result of running this code (available as *array_pop.htm* in the companion archive) is shown in Figure 7-6, where you can see that the value `'Tortoiseshell'` was popped off the array, and underneath all the remaining elements are displayed, confirming that the previous final element has now been removed.

Using `array_push()` and `array_pop()` Together

The `array_pop()` function is most commonly used with `array_push()` when writing code that uses recursion. Recursion is any section of code that calls itself, and which can then call itself again, and keep on doing so until the task of the code is complete (it's like *Inception* yet again!).

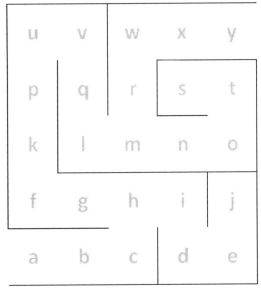

Figure 7: A simple 5 × 5 maze.

If this sounds complicated consider a search algorithm for exploring a maze such as the one in Figure 7-7, in which the objective is to find your way from the starting point at a to the finish at y.

You can clearly see the path to follow, but a computer is not so smart and will need to investigate the maze as if it's a rat, with walls higher than it can see over. Therefore a program to do this will easily find its way along the path a-b-c-h, but then it will encounter a choice of going either left to location (or cell) g, or right to i.

Let's assume it chooses the latter after selecting a direction at random. The program will then follow the path i-d-e-j, only to encounter a dead end, requiring the program to return. Let's look at tracking this entire path so far using the push() function:

```php
$Maze = array();
array_push($Maze, 'a');
array_push($Maze, 'b');
array_push($Maze, 'c');
array_push($Maze, 'h');
array_push($Maze, 'i');
array_push($Maze, 'd');
```

```
array_push($Maze, 'e');
array_push($Maze, 'j');
```

If you assume that there's also some extra code (not documented here) that knows which cells it has and hasn't yet visited, the program can now use the simple method of popping each cell off the array until it reaches one where it can get to a cell not yet visited. Pseudo-code (the actions to take expressed in plain English) to do this might look as follows:

```
While no unvisited cell is accessible
    pop a location off the array
```

And the sequence of actions that would happen within the loop section of this code would be like this:

```
$Location = array_pop($Maze); // Returns 'j'
```

Since no unvisited cell can be reached from 'j' (as determined by the code that we assume is there but not documented) the loop will go round again, and again, until an unvisited cell can be accessed, resulting in four additional calls to array_pop(), as follows:

```
$Location = array_pop($Maze); // Returns 'e'
$Location = array_pop($Maze); // Returns 'd'
$Location = array_pop($Maze); // Returns 'i'
$Location = array_pop($Maze); // Returns 'h'
```

Now, when the program finds it has popped the location 'h' off the stack, it discovers there's a new cell it can go to, namely 'g', and so the process continues along the path g-f-k-p-u-v-q-l-m, at which point another choice of directions is encountered: either 'r' or 'n'.

To track this path the program will push all the cells between 'g' and 'm' onto the array, and then also push the path n-o-t-s, at which point another dead end is encountered.

Then, as before, the code pops off all the cells in a loop until it reaches 'm', at which point the unvisited cell 'r' is accessible and the final path out of the maze is discovered: r-w-x-y.

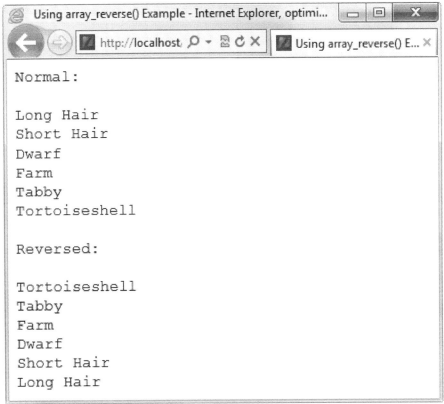

Figure 8: Array elements before and after reversing.

Note: *Recursion is quite complex programming, especially for beginners, which is why I have not documented the ancillary code you would use to take care of tracking the visited and unvisited cells. I simply wanted to offer a visual example of recursion that would explain what's going on, and show how to use* array_push() *and* array_pop() *together. But don't worry if you find any of it confusing, as you can safely move on with the course and come back here another time, when you find an actual need for these functions.*

Using `array_reverse()`

When you want to reverse the order of elements in an array you can call the `array_reverse()` function, which actually reverses the array contents, rather than returning a new array as some other functions do.

To use the function simply attach it to the array to be reversed, like this:

```
$MyArray = array_reverse($MyArray);
```

Figure 7-8 shows this function being used to reverse the $Cats[] array from previous examples, the code for which is available as *array_reverse.htm* in the companion archive.

Using FILO and FIFO Arrays

The array_reverse() function is sometimes used on an array of elements that have been created by popping the values onto it. As you will know from the earlier array_push() section, pushed values are added to the end of an array such that when you come to pop them off again they are returned in reverse order. This is often referred to as a FILO (First In / Last Out) array. When an array is used this way it is also sometimes called a *stack*.

But if you wish to operate a FIFO (First In / First Out) stack, you can reverse an array before pushing an item onto it and then reverse it again ready for elements to be popped off. That way the first value pushed onto it will be the first one popped off, and so on.

This type of array or stack is also known as a *buffer*, and is typically used for handling events such as keyboard input, in which the key presses should be stored (buffered) until needed, and returned in the order they were pressed.

Buffering Using an Array

You can see a simulation of this in the following code, in which the word 'Fred' is being pushed into the array $Buffer(), with the array's contents shown in the comment immediately following each statement. The top (or start) of the array is at the left of the string shown in the comments, and the bottom (or end) of the array (onto which values are pushed and popped) is at the right of the string:

```
$Buffer = array_reverse($Buffer); // $Buffer = ''
array_push($Buffer, 'F');          // $Buffer = 'F'
$Buffer = array_reverse($Buffer); // $Buffer = 'F'

$Buffer = array_reverse($Buffer); // $Buffer = 'F'
array_push($Buffer, 'r');          // $Buffer = 'Fr'
$Buffer = array_reverse($Buffer); // $Buffer = 'rF'
```

```
$Buffer = array_reverse($Buffer);  // $Buffer = 'Fr'
array_push($Buffer, 'e');          // $Buffer = 'Fre'
$Buffer = array_reverse($Buffer);  // $Buffer = 'erF'


$Buffer = array_reverse($Buffer);  // $Buffer = 'Fre'
array_push($Buffer, 'd');          // $Buffer = 'Fred'
$Buffer = array_reverse($Buffer);  // $Buffer = 'derF'
```

Initially `$Buffer()` is empty and has no elements, but then the letter 'F' is pushed onto it. Seeing as the array has only a single element, reversing it at this point has no effect. However, when the next letter, 'r', is to be added it is pushed to the bottom of the array, denoted in the comment as being on the right of the 'F'.

After reversing the array back again the 'r' is at the top and 'F' is at the bottom of the array. This is exactly where we want them because if the code that uses this buffering system is ready to process the next key press in the buffer, it can simply issue a call to `array_pop()`, which will pull the letter 'F' off it. This is correct because when processing buffered data such as this, the letters typed must be processed in the order typed.

When the letter 'e' is processed the array is once again reversed so that it can be added to the bottom of the array, then the array is reversed back again so that should `array_pop()` be called at *this* point, 'F' will be the first letter popped off. After this third set of statements 'F' is at the bottom of the array, 'r' is in the middle, and 'e' is at the top.

Finally the letter 'd' is processed using the same procedure so that after it has been placed in the array it is at the top, with the 'F' at the bottom.

You can also 'push' values to the start (instead of the end) of an array using the (curiously named) `array_unshift()` function. Likewise you can 'pop' from the end of an array using the `array_shift()` function.

Note: *But let's not get too far ahead of ourselves quite yet, as there are a couple more array functions to introduce, before getting to creating your own functions in the following Lecture.*

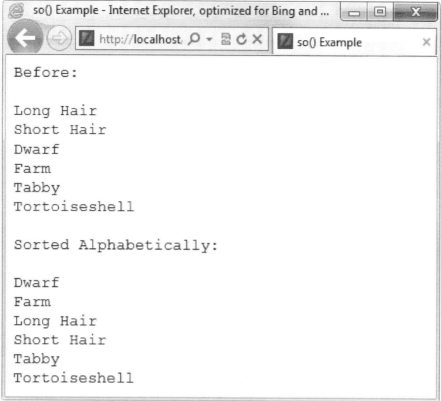

Figure 9: Sorting an array alphabetically.

Using `sort()`

PHP comes with a handy `sort()` function to sort arrays alphabetically in descending order. This function changes the actual array to which it is applied, unlike some other functions that simply return a new array, leaving the original untouched.

To sort an array simply call the `sort()` function, passing it the array to be sorted, as with this example that uses the `$Cats[]` array:

```
$Cats = array('Long Hair', 'Short Hair', 'Dwarf',
            'Farm',       'Tabby',       'Tortoiseshell');
sort($Cats);
```

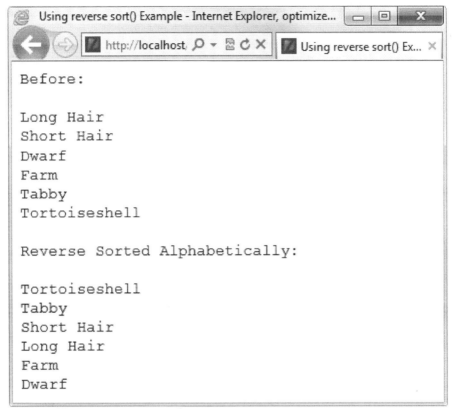

Figure 10: Reversing a sorted array.

The result of issuing this `sort()` call (the code for which is available as *sort.php* in the companion archive) is shown in Figure 7-9.

If all you require is an alphabetical sort in ascending order then `sort()` is just the function for you. However, should you need to sort an array numerically then you need to pass the specifier `SORT_NUMERIC` to the `sort()` function, like this:

```
sort($NumericArray, SORT_NUMERIC);
```

Reversing a Sort

To obtain a reversed sort of any kind (alphabetic, numeric and so on) all you need to do is pass the sorted array to the `array_reverse()` function, like this (as shown in Figure 7-10):

```
sort($Cats);
$Cats = array_reverse($Cats);
```

Using `splice()`

I've left possibly the most powerful array function, `array_splice()`, until last because you can use it to provide the same facility as most of the other array functions, and a lot more too.

With `array_splice()` you can remove one or more elements from an array, or insert one or more into an array, and you can do either at any position within the array. What's more, you can remove and insert at the same time, providing a replace facility that can swap one or more elements with more, the same or fewer elements.

Removing Elements From an Array

Let's look first at how to remove one or more elements from an array, starting with the `$Cats[]` array we've been using a lot. In the following example the `array_splice()` function is called with two arguments. The first is the element at which to perform the splice (starting from 0), and the second is the number of elements to be removed:

```
$Cats = array('Long Hair', 'Short Hair', 'Dwarf',
              'Farm',      'Tabby',      'Tortoiseshell');
array_splice($Cats, 2, 3);
```

Therefore, with arguments of 2 and 3, the splice starts at the element index 2, which is the third one, and the second argument of 3 states that three elements are to be removed from the array.

If you need to know which elements have been removed you can access the result of calling the function, which is an array containing the removed elements, like this:

```
$Removed = array_splice($Cats, 2, 3);
```

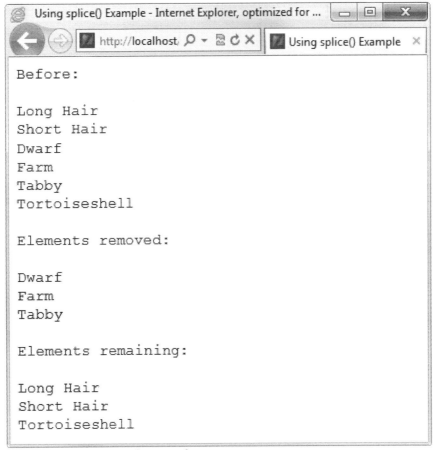

Figure 11: Removing elements from an array.

Figure 7-11 shows this code brought together, displaying the array before splicing, the elements removed by the splice, and the elements remaining afterwards.

Inserting Elements Into an Array

Using a similar call to `array_splice()` you can insert new values into the array, as in the following example, which adds two more breeds of cat starting at the third element:

```
array_splice($Cats, 2, 0, array('Siamese', 'Persian'));
```

Here, the first argument following the `$Cats[]` array is the third element in the array, and the following argument of 0 tells `array_splice()` there are no elements to be removed.

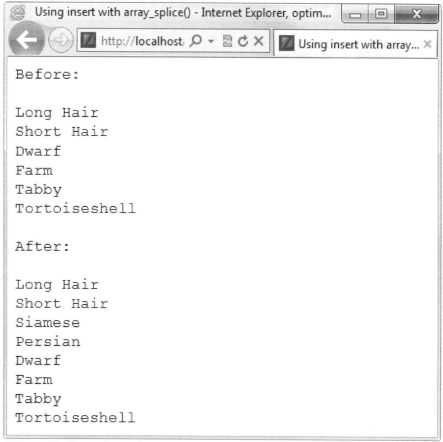

Figure 12: Inserting values into an array.

After this there is an array containing two new arguments, which tells `array_splice()` to insert these elements into the `$Cats[]` array starting at element 2 (the third one). You may place as many values as you like here to insert as many new elements as you need. The result of making this call is shown in Figure 7-12.

Advanced Array Splicing

Finally, you can remove and insert elements at the same time using a call such as the following:

```
$Results = array_splice($Cats, 2, 3, array('Siamese', 'Persian'));
```

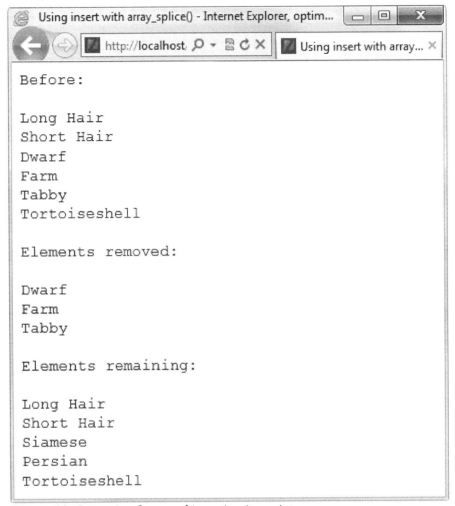

Figure 13: Removing from and inserting items into an array.

This statement tells `array_splice()` to use a splice index of 2 (the third element), at which location it must remove three elements, and then insert the new values supplied. The result of issuing this call is shown in Figure 7-13.

Example files are available in the companion archive demonstrating all three types of splicing. They are *array_splice.htm*, *insert_array_splice.htm* and *advanced_array_splice.htm*.

Summary

You now know how to use all types of PHP array, whether single or multi-dimensional, numeric, string, associative or otherwise. Coupled with your earlier knowledge of variables and operators you are now ready to really get down to power programming, beginning with the following lecture on controlling program flow.

CONTROLLING PROGRAM FLOW

By following this lecture you will:

- ✓ *Learn how to change the flow of program execution..*
- ✓ *Understand how to use conditional statements.*
- ✓ *Know how to best handle long lists of options.*

HAVING REACHED THIS point in the course you've actually already learned the vast majority of PHP. You should understand how to incorporate it into a web page, the syntax to use, handling numeric variables, strings and arrays, using operators in expressions according to their associativity, and you've even learned the basics of handling program flow control using the `if()` and `else` keywords.

In this lecture you'll consolidate your knowledge of the latter so that you can precisely control the flow of program execution.

The `if()` Statement

You've already seen this statement in use a few times, but only with single line statements, so here's the full syntax of an `if()` statement:

```
if (expression)
{
    // Execute this code, which can be one...
```

```
        // ...or more lines
    }
```

In this example expression can be any expression at all created using numbers, strings, variables, objects and operators. The result of the expression must be a Boolean value that can be either TRUE or FALSE, such as if ($MyVar > 7) ..., and so on.

The curly braces encapsulate the code that must be executed upon the expression evaluating to TRUE, and there can be none, one, or many statements.

Omitting the Braces

To enable you to create short and simple if() statements without having to use braces, they are optional if only one statement is to be executed upon the expression being TRUE, like this:

```
    if ($Time < 12) echo 'Good morning';
```

If the code to execute is quite long (so that it might wrap to the following line) you may wish to start it on the following line, but if you do so, because no curly braces are being used to encapsulate the statement, it's best to indent the statement by a few spaces or a tab, so that it clearly belongs to the if() statement, like this:

```
    if (Time < 12)
        echo 'Good morning. How are you today?';
```

Indeed, if you have a really long statement to execute it can also be a good idea to split it over several lines at suitable points, like this:

```
    if ($Time < 12)
        echo 'Good morning. Following is the list "  .
            'of all your appointments for today. The " .
            'important ones are highlighted in bold';
```

Here I have split the output into three parts by breaking it into three strings, which are displayed one after the other using . operators. I also further indented the follow on lines to clearly indicate that they belong to the echo command.

However, in my view this has become a borderline case where you might be better advised to encapsulate the statement within curly braces, because they will ensure there is no ambiguity, and you won't have worry about the wrapping of long lines diminishing the code readability, like this:

```
if ($Time < 12)

{

   echo 'Good morning. Following is the list of all your

appointments for today. The important ones are highlighted

in bold';

}
```

Some program editors will automatically indent wrapped around lines for you (based on the indent at the start of the line) making the code even more readable, and looking like this:

```
if ($Time < 12)

{

   echo 'Good morning. Following is the list of all your

   appointments for today. The important ones are highlighted

   in bold';

}
```

Note: In this latter case, the program editor will treat all three lines of the statement as a single line, which they are. Don't try to format your code like this using newlines, though, as it will split it into multiple lines and cause errors – unless you also break the statement into parts, as detailed earlier.

Positioning of Braces

The reason you can lay out your code in a variety of ways is that PHP supports the use of tabs, spaces and newlines as *whitespace*, which is ignored. Because of this programmers can choose to place the curly braces wherever they like. As you have seen, when I use them I generally place the opening and closing brace directly under the if() statement's first character, and then indent the encapsulated statements, like this:

```
if (expression)
{
  // Execute this code, which can be one...
  // ...or more lines
}
```

Other programmers, however, choose to place the opening curly brace immediately after the `if()`, like this:

```
if (expression) {
  // Execute this code, which can be one...
  // ...or more lines
}
```

Both of these (and other) types of layout (such as leaving the closing curly brace at the end of the final statement) are perfectly acceptable.

Note: There are also some less-used layouts used by other programmers, but the preceding tend to be the main two. I advocate the first type because (even though it requires an extra line of code for each opening brace) it makes the opening braces indent to the level of the closing ones, so that if you have several nested statements, you can more clearly determine that you have the right number of opening and closing braces, and that they are all in the right places. It also places more vertical whitespace between the expression and the statements that follow, which I find helpful. However, which system you use is entirely up to you.

The `else` Statement

To accompany the `if()` statement there's also an `else` keyword, which follows the same rules as `if()`, except the code following an `else` is executed only if the expression following the `if()` evaluates to FALSE.

If the code comprises a single statement it doesn't require encapsulating in curly braces, but if it has two or more statements braces are required.

You use the `else` keyword in conjunction with `if()`, like this:

```
if ($Age < 18)

{

  echo 'You are not an adult.';

}

else

{

  echo 'You are an adult.';

}
```

Since both of these keywords only include a single statement you can safely omit the braces if you wish, like this:

```
if ($Age < 18)

  echo 'You are not an adult.';

else

  echo 'You are an adult.';
```

Or, if there's room, you can even move the statements up to directly follow the keywords, like this:

```
if ($Age < 18) echo 'You are not an adult.');

else            echo 'You are an adult.';
```

Note: In this instance I opted to indent the second statement until it lined up underneath the first one. This helps make it clear what's going on at a glance if I were to come back to this code some months later. However, how you lay out your whitespace is entirely up to you.

There is another convention regarding braces that I recommend you consider using, which is that if one of the statements in an if() ... else construct uses braces, then so should the other, even if the other one only has a single statement. You can see the difference in the following (all valid) examples, in which I think you'll find that Example 3 (with both sets of statements in braces) is the easiest to follow:

```
if ($Age < 18) // Example 1
{
  echo 'You are not an adult. ';
  echo 'Sorry, you cannot vote yet.';
}
else
  echo 'You are an adult.';


if ($Age < 18) // Example 2
  echo 'You are not an adult. ';
else
{
  echo 'You are an adult. ';
  echo 'You can vote.';
}


if ($Age < 18) // Example 3
{
  echo 'You are not an adult. ';
  echo 'Sorry, you cannot vote yet.';
}
else
{
 echo 'You are an adult.';
}
```

You don't *have* to follow this advice, but it will certainly make your debugging a lot easier if you do, and any other programmers who have to maintain your code will thank you for it.

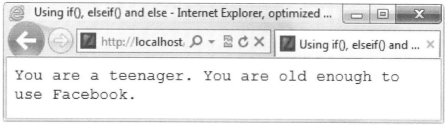

Figure 1: Using multiple `else if()` statements.

The `elseif()` statement

You can extend the power of `if()` … `else` even further by also incorporating `elseif()` statements, which provide a third option to the original `if()` statement, and which you place before the final `else` statement (if there is one).

The following example illustrates how you might use this keyword:

```
if ($Value < 0)       echo 'Negative';
elseif ($Value > 0) echo 'Positive';
else                    echo 'Zero';
```

Note: As with other examples, I have used whitespace liberally in the preceding code to line the statements up and make them easier to follow.

The `elseif()` statement follows the same rules as the `if()` and `else` statements with regard to using curly braces to encapsulate multiple statements (but not requiring them for single statements). However I give the same recommendation as I did earlier that if even one of the parts of an `if()` … `elseif()` … `else` structure uses braces, then I advise you to use braces for all parts.

Of course, you don't have to use a concluding `else` after an `if()` … `elseif()` construct if you don't want it. For example, if you don't need to deal with the case of a zero value (perhaps because one is not possible in the code you have written), you might simply use the following:

```
if ($Value < 0)       echo 'Negative';
elseif ($Value > 0) echo 'Positive';
```

Note: *The purpose of the* else *keyword is as a catch-all, to trap all possible values that remain and execute the statement(s) attached to it if none of the preceding statements in the clause are* TRUE.

The switch() Statement

The if(), elseif() and else statements are very powerful, and comprise much of PHP programming. But they are not the most efficient method of controlling program flow when there are more than three options to consider. For example, imagine there's an input field on the web page with the following string values from which the user must select their age range:

- 0-1
- 2-3
- 4-6
- 7-12
- 13-17
- 18+

Now here's some code you might use to process the value returned by the input, as shown in Figure 8-1 in which a value of '13-17' has been pre-selected for the string variable $Age (using the *if_else.php* file from the companion archive):

```php
$Age = '13-17';


if ($Age == '0-1')

{

        echo 'You are a baby. ';

        echo 'How can you read this?';

}
else if ($Age == '2-3')

{

        echo 'You are a toddler.';

}
else if ($Age == '4-6')

{
```

```
        echo 'You are an infant. ';
        echo 'You go to nursery or school.';
}
else if ($Age == '7-12')
{
        echo 'You are a child.';
}
else if ($Age == '13-17'

{
        echo 'You are a teenager. ';
        echo 'You are old enough to use Facebook.';
}
else echo 'You are an adult.';
```

Don't you think all those repeated `elseif()` statement are rather cumbersome, and the code feels somewhat heavier than it could be?

Well the answer is to restructure code such as this using a `switch()` statement in conjunction with the `case` and `break` keywords, like this (as shown in Figure 8-2, created using the *switch.php* file from the companion archive, and in which the string `$Age` is pre-assigned the value `'4-6'`):

```
$Age = '4-6';

switch($Age)
{
  case '0-1':   echo 'You are a baby. ';
                echo 'How can you read this?';
                break;
  case '2-3':   echo 'You are a toddler.';
                break;
  case '4-6':   echo 'You are an infant. ';
```

```
                      echo 'You go to nursery or school.';
                      break;
    case '7-12':      echo 'You are a child.';
                      break;
    case '13-17':     echo 'You are a teenager. ';
                      echo 'You can use Facebook.';
    default:          echo 'You are an adult.';
  }
```

I'm sure you'll agree that using switch() statements is a lot clearer than a set of sprawling elseif()s. To use one, simply place the expression or variable to be tested in the brackets following the switch keyword, then within a pair of curly braces (which are required), provide a number of case statements and an optional default statement.

Following each case keyword place one possible value that the switch variable or expression might have. In this example $Age can only have string values, but you can equally test for digits or floating point numbers too. After the possible value place a colon followed by the statements to execute if the value matches the switch variable or expression. In this example it's one or more echo statements.

Note: Note how no curly braces are required to contain multiple statements. This is because, once the code following the colon starts executing, it will keep on going, executing statement after statement (ignoring the case tests), until the closing curly brace at the end of the switch() statement is encountered.

Using the **break** Keyword

Because program flow will continue to the end of a switch() statement (executing all the remaining statements regardless of any case keywords encountered) you must mark the end of a sequence of statements to be executed with a break keyword. This causes program flow to jump to just after the closing brace of the switch() statement.

Note: You will also encounter the break keyword in Lecture 9 where it is used to break to the end of looping structures of code.

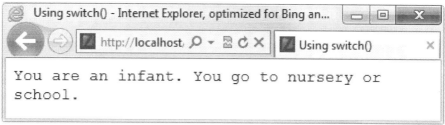

Figure 2: Using a `switch()` *statement.*

Using the `default` Keyword

In the same way that the `else` keyword is a catch-all device for dealing with any other values not caught by `if()` or `elseif()` statements, you can use the `default` keyword within a `switch()` statement to catch any values not matched by the `case` statements.

In the previous example, since all possible values for `$Age` are tested for except for `'18+'`, then if none of the case statements match, `$Age` must contain the value `'18+'`. Therefore the `default` statement is triggered and the statement following it writes the string `'You are an adult.'` to the browser.

Note: *There is no* `break` *keyword after the* `default` *option in the preceding example because it is the last statement in the* `switch()` *statement, and therefore a* `break` *keyword is superfluous in this position, as it would only add extra, unnecessary code. There is, however, nothing stopping you placing the* `default` *statement anywhere within a* `switch()` *statement (even at the start), but if you do so you must add a* `break` *keyword after the statements it executes, or program flow will fall through to the following statements, rather than to the end of the* `switch()` *statement.*

Allowing Fall-through

Sometimes you may not want to use the `break` keyword because you wish to allow cases to fall-through to other cases. For example, consider the case of wanting to choose the correct language to display on a multi-national website. Using a simple input field (or even a geolocation program if you want to be really smart) you could return a string containing the user's country name, for example, perhaps out of the following:

- `Australia`
- `Brazil`
- `France`
- `Germany`

- Portugal
- Spain
- UK
- USA

Then code to process the country name in the variable $Country to a language to use in the variable $Language might look like this:

```
switch($Country)
{
   case 'Australia':
   case 'UK':
   case 'USA':
   default:         $Language = 'English';
                    break;
   case 'Brazil':
   case 'Portugal': $Language = 'Portuguese';
                    break;
   case 'France':   $Language = 'French';
                    break;
   case 'Germany':  $Language = 'German';
                    break;
   case 'Spain':    $Language = 'Spanish';
}
```

Only after the variable $Language has been assigned its value is the break keyword used. So if any of the countries 'Australia', 'UK' or 'USA' are selected, then $Language is set to 'English', which is also selected (because the default keyword is included within the fall-through group of cases) for any other value not tested for by the cases in the switch() statement.

A fall-through also occurs for 'Brazil' and 'Portugal', both of which countries speak 'Portuguese', but the remaining countries have different languages and don't use any `case` fall-throughs. Note that there is no `break` keyword after the final statement as it is not needed because the end of the `switch()` has already been reached.

Note: *Yes I know that many people in the USA speak Spanish, but this is simply an example to explain fall-through. If you wanted to cater for that option, though, you could have two country names for the USA:* `'USA English'` *and* `'USA Spanish'`*, and then simply add a fall-through to the* `'Spain'` *case – while you are at it you could also add* `'Canada English'` *and* `'Canada French'` *in a similar fashion to cater for its two languages, and so on.*

Summary

This lecture concludes everything you need to know to write basic PHP programs. You can now handle data in various ways, including variables and arrays, you are able to use complex operators and expressions, and now you can direct the flow of your programs. In the next Lecture, therefore, we'll start to look at more advanced aspects of PHP, beginning with putting together various types of looping constructs.

LOOPING SECTIONS OF CODE

By following this lecture you will:

- ✓ *Learn the power of using loops for repetitive tasks.*
- ✓ *Discover the different types of loop structures available.*
- ✓ *Know how to break out of a loop when necessary.*

IN THE PREVIOUS lecture you learned all about program flow control, branching, and using `if()`, `else` and `switch()` statements. These are perfect for altering the program flow according to values and expressions, but not so good when you need to repetitively execute a process, such as processing a document a word at a time to find typographical errors.

This is the type of situation where PHP's looping statements come into their own. With them you form a loop around a core group of statements and then keep the loop circulating until (or unless) one or more conditions are met such as (in the case of a spelling checker) when the end of the document is reached.

More than that, the different loop types supported also enable you to pre-assign values to variables used in the loop, or only enter into a loop if a certain expression is satisfied.

Using `while()` Loops

The `while()` statement provides the simplest type of PHP loop. In English what it does is something like this: "While such-and-such is true then keep doing so-and-so until such-and-such is no-longer true, or forever if such-and-such is never true". Here's an example that will display the ten times table (as shown in Figure 9-1):

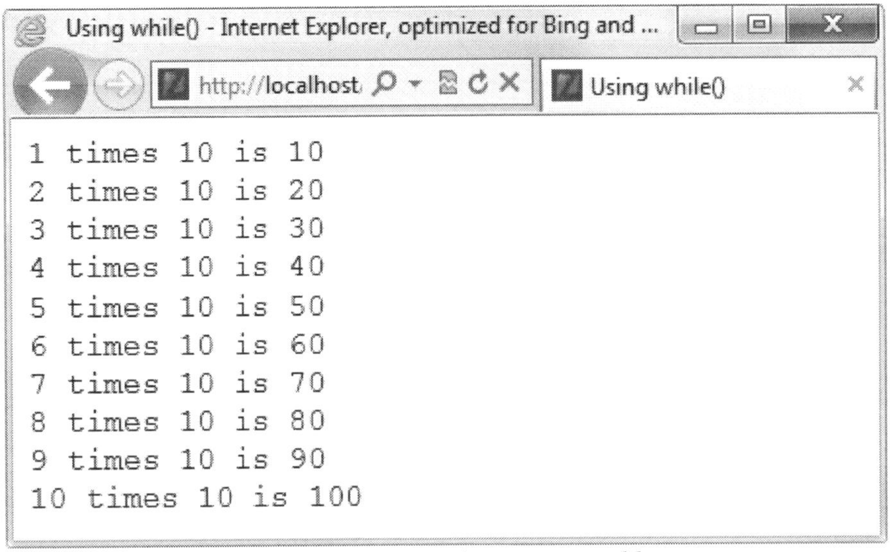

Figure 1: Using `while()` *to calculate the 10 times table.*

```
$j = 0;

while ($j++ < 10)
{
    echo "$j times 10 is " . $j * 10 . '<br />';
}
```

The code used for this and the other examples in this lecture is available in the files *while.php*, *do_while.php. for.php*, *break.php*, and *continue.php* in the companion archive.

The Example in Detail

This code starts by initializing the variable `$j` to 0. This variable is used both to decide when to loop (and when to stop looping) and also for calculating the times table. Then the `while()` statement tests for `$j` having a value of less than 10. The first time around its value is 0 so the expression evaluates to TRUE. Note also that `$j` is post-incremented after making the test by using the ++ increment operator. This means that the second time around the loop `$j` will have a value of 1:

```
while ($j++ < 10)
```

Inside the braces there is a single statement, which prints the value in $j, some text and then the result of multiplying $j by 10. Since $j was post-incremented after the test at the start of the loop, it now has a value of 1, so the sentence '1 times 10 is 10' is output to the browser:

```
echo "$j times 10 is " . $j * 10 . '<br />';
```

After the echo statement is executed the end of the loop is reached and so program flow returns to the start of the loop once more, where $j is once again tested for having a value less than 10.

This time around it now has a value of 1, so that satisfies the test, and then $j is post-incremented, giving it a value of 2. Therefore, this time around the loop, $j has a value of 2 and so the sentence '2 times 10 is 20' is output to the browser, and the loop goes round another time.

This process continues until $j has a value of 10, and the test at the start of the loop therefore no-longer results in TRUE, so program execution jumps to just after the closing brace of the while() statement.

Note: *Since there is only a single statement inside this loop, just as with* `for()` *statements, you can omit the curly braces if you wish, like this:*

```
while ($j++ < 10)
    echo "$j times 10 is " . $j * 10 . '<br />';
```

Using do … while() Loops

With a while() loop, if the test at the start is not satisfied, program execution will not flow into the loop. Sometimes, however, you want program flow to go around a loop at least once, in which case it's necessary to perform the loop test afterward.

For example, suppose you wish to calculate the factorial of the number 10 (sometimes displayed mathematically as 10!). This involves multiplying all the numbers from 1 to 10 together, like this: $10 \times 9 \times 8 \times 7 \times 6 \times 5 \times 4 \times 3 \times 2 \times 1$.

Using a loop to do this is an efficient method of calculating this value, particularly since once the loop has been built, it can be used to calculate the factorial of any number. And one thing we know for sure about this loop is that it will execute at least once. Therefore a `do … while()` structure may be best suited, and you can achieve that like this:

```
$j = 10;
$f = 1;

do
{
  $f *= $j--;
} while ($j > 0);

echo '10! is ' . $f;
```

One of the neat things about this loop is that `$f` always contains the running total of all previous multiplications, so all that's necessary to do in each iteration is multiply `$f` by the current value in `$j`, save that value back into `$f` and then decrement `$j`, which is performed by this statement:

```
$f *= $j--;
```

As you will see, the `*=` assignment operator is ideal in this situation, because it performs both the multiplication and the assignment of the result back to `$f` using a single operator. Also the post-decrement operator applied to `$j` makes for more efficient coding too.

The Example in Detail

In detail what occurs in the preceding example is that `$j` is a loop counter which is initialized to the value 10 (because there are ten numbers to multiply) and `$f` is the factorial, which is initialized to 1, since the loop will start with the expression `$f *= $j--;`, which the first time around the loop will be the equivalent of `$f = 1 * 10;`.

The post-decrement operator after the `$j` ensures that each time around the loop the multiplier is decremented by one (but only after the value in `$j` is used in the expression). So, the second time around the loop, `$f` will now have a value of 10, and `$j` will be 9, so the expression will be equivalent to `$f = 10 * 9;`.

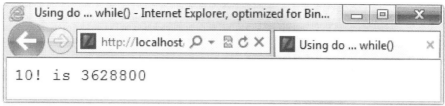

Figure 2: Using `do ... while()` *to calculate the factorial of a number.*

Then on the next iteration, `$f` will have a value of `90` as it enters the loop, and `$j` will be 8, so the these two values will be multiplied together and placed back into `$f`. The expressions evaluated in the loop are therefore as follows:

```
$f =        1 * 10; // Results in 10
$f =       10 *  9; // Results in 90
$f =       90 *  8; // Results in 720
$f =      720 *  7; // Results in 5040
$f =     5040 *  6; // Results in 30240
$f =    30240 *  5; // Results in 151200
$f =   151200 *  4; // Results in 604800
$f =   604800 *  3; // Results in 1314400
$f = 1814400 *  2; // Results in 3628800
$f = 3628800 *  1; // Results in 3628800
```

When the expression at the end of the loop (in the `while()` part) evaluates to `FALSE`, this means that `$j` is no-longer greater than 0, and so the loop is not re-entered, and program flow continues at the first instruction following the loop.

When this example is loaded into a browser (as shown in Figure 9-2), the result shown in the final line is displayed, by the `echo` instruction that follows the loop.

Note: *As with many other PHP constructs, if there is only one statement inside the loop, you can omit the curly braces if you like, and the loop could therefore be written like this:*

```
do $f *= $j--;
while ($j > 0);
```

Using `for()` Loops

Although the preceding to types of loop structure may seem sufficient for most requirements, they can actually be improved on, especially since you must first initialize

variables outside of these loops before they are even entered, and then you generally have
to increment or decrement at least one variable inside the loop, too.

For these reasons a third type of loop structure is supported, the `for()` loop, and it is one
of the most compact and most-used forms of loop structure for these reasons:

- It allows you to initialize all the variables you need, within the creation of the
  loop.
- It allows you specify the test condition within the creation of the loop.
- It allows you to specify variables to change after each loop iteration within the
  creation of the loop.

Let's look at how you can do this by rewriting the previous example, as follows:

```
for ($j = 10, $f = 1 ; $j > 0 ; --$j)
{
    $f *= $j;
}


echo "10! is $f";
```

Doesn't that look much simpler than the `do ... while()` version? As before there's still a
single statement inside the loop, but it no-longer uses the post-decrement operator,
because `$j` is decremented within the set-up section of the loop. Also there are no
variables pre-assigned outside of the loop, because that is also handled within the loop set-
up.

The Example in Detail

Here's what's going on. A `for()` loop's set-up section (the part within brackets) is divided
into three parts which are separated with semicolons. Each part performs the following, in
order:

1. Initializes any variables used within the loop.
2. Performs a test to see whether the loop should be entered.
3. Changes any variables required after each loop iteration.

The first and third sections may include more than one statement as long as you separate them using commas. Therefore in the first section of the preceding example, $j is initialized to a value of 10, and $f to a value of 1, like this:

```
$j = 10, $f = 1
```

Next comes the loop test:

```
$j > 0
```

And finally $j is post-decremented:

```
--$j
```

With the three sets of arguments inside the brackets looking like this:

```
$j = 10, $f = 1 ; $j > 0 ; --$j
```

And that's really all there is too it. When the loop is first entered the variables are initialized. This will not happen in any other iterations. Then the test in part two of the loop set-up is made, and if the expression evaluates to TRUE, the loop is entered.

Next the expressions in the loop are executed (in this case there's only one), and then the third section of the loop set-up is executed, which in this case decrements $j. Then, the second time and all subsequent times around the loop, section one of the set-up section is skipped and program flow goes straight to the test in section two.

If this is TRUE then the loop is again entered, the statements in it executed, and then the statements in the third part of the set-up section are executed and the loop goes around again. But if the test doesn't evaluate to TRUE then program flow goes to the code following the loop, which in this case is the echo statement, to print the calculated factorial value.

Note: Since there is only a single statement within the loop of the preceding example the braces may legally be omitted from the code, like this (or you can make the code even more compact by placing the statement directly after the loop section):

```
for ($j = 10, $f = 1; $j > 0 ; --$j)
   $f *= $j;
```

Generally `for()` loops are so powerful that they have become widespread and you will very rarely find that you need to use a `while()` or `do … while()` loop, because `for()` loops can compactly and neatly accomplish almost every type of looping structure you could want in PHP.

Breaking Out Of a Loop

Amazingly I still haven't yet finished introducing you to everything that PHP loops can do for you, because there's still the matter of a couple of keywords you can employ to further enhance their use.

The first of these is the `break` keyword, which I already showed being used with `switch()` statement in Lecture 8 to stop fall-through of program flow between cases. But the `break` keyword is not exclusive to `switch()` statements. In fact it can also be used inside loops too.

But why would you want to use a `break` within a loop? Surely you have all the tests for conditions you could want already? Well, not quite, as it turns out. Sometimes you may want to terminate a loop early, as with the following example, which searches an array for a particular value:

```
$HayStack = array(1, 23, 16.3, 88.23, 11, 24.46, 30, 99);
$Needle   = 11;

echo "Searching for $Needle: ";

for ($j = 0 ; $j < sizeof($HayStack) ; ++$j)
{
   if ($HayStack[$j] == $Needle) break;
}
```

```
        if ($j < sizeof($HayStack)) echo "Found at index $j";
        else                        echo 'Not found';
```

If the value being searched for is found then it would be a waste of time to continue searching the array (unless multiple occurrences are been looked for), and so terminating the loop early makes sense. And this is done with a `break` statement, as shown in Figure 9-3.

As with other PHP structures, since this example has only a single statement in the loop, the braces can be omitted for simplicity, like this:

```
        for ($j = 0 ; $j < sizeof($HayStack) ; ++$j)
          if ($HayStack[$j] == $Needle) break;
```

Note: When you use the `break` *keyword within a loop that is itself inside one or more other loops, only the current loop will be broken out from, because the* `break` *keyword applies only to the scope of the current object in which it exists.*

The `continue` Statement

The `break` statement diverts flow to the statement immediately following the loop in which it exists, but sometimes this is too drastic a measure, because you may only want to skip the current iteration of a loop, and not all remaining iterations.

When this is the case you can use the `continue` statement, which forces program flow to skip over any remaining statements in a loop, and to start again at the next iteration of the loop. One reason for wanting to do this might be (for example) to avoid encountering a division by zero error, which could generate invalid results.

For example, consider the case of some code that must calculate the reciprocal of all numbers between -5 and 5. The reciprocal of a number is found by dividing the value 1 by that number.

So if the number happens to be zero an attempt would be made to divide 1 by 0, which in PHP results in the value infinity, which is not a useful number in this context, so we need to check for it and remove the possibility, like this:

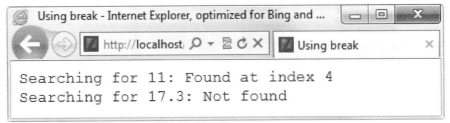

Figure 3: Using break to exit from a loop if a condition is met.

```
for ($j = -5 ; $j < 6 ; ++$j)

{

    if ($j == 0) continue;


    echo "1/$j is " . 1 / $j . '<br />';

}
```

Figure 9-4 shows this code being run in a browser. As you can see, when the value 0 is reached for $j, nothing is displayed, because the continue keyword has forced the loop to skip to its next iteration.

Summary

Now that you know how to use the wide variety of looping structures provided by PHP, you can begin to develop your own programming style, because it's now possible for you to write most types of code that rely on loops in a number of different ways, and before long you will begin to settle on the structures that fit your way of thinking the best.

For example, most programmers tend to generally use for() loops, but then they may need to occasionally use the break keyword for special instances. Whereas those who prefer while() and do … while() loops rarely need to use break. It's a matter of personal style.

Anyway, whichever types of loop structures you find yourself migrating towards, in the next lecture you'll discover even more powerful things you can do with PHP, including writing functions and using global and local variables.

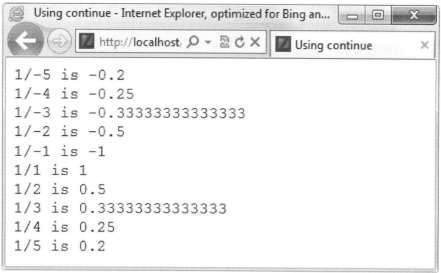

Figure 4: Using `continue` *to skip a loop iteration.*

PHP FUNCTIONS

By following this lecture you will:

- ✓ *Be able to create your own functions.*
- ✓ *Know how to pass values to and from functions.*
- ✓ *Understand the difference between local and global scope.*

AS WELL AS using conditional statements such as if() and switch() and loops such as while() and for() there's another way you can control program flow called the *function*. Functions are sections of code that you call from any other part of code (or even the function itself, which is known as recursion), and which then perform one or more actions and then return.

When functions return they may also return a value back to the calling code, or they can simply return without doing so, in which case the returned value will be undefined. Interestingly, as you will learn in the following lecture, in PHP functions are also objects so they can be passed as values, used in arrays and so on.

Using Functions

PHP comes with many in-built functions. For example, to obtain the square root of the number 49 you can call the sqrt() function, like this, which will return the value 7:

```
echo sqrt(49);
```

The optional value you pass to a function is called an argument, and you can have any number of these arguments, or none. In the case of sqrt() a single value is required. The square root of that number is then calculated, and the value derived is returned. That's how the `echo` command in the preceding example can display the square root value, because that value is returned directly to the calling code, which is the `echo` statement.

You create functions using the keyword `function`, followed by the name to give to the function, and then a pair of brackets, within which you list the arguments being passed to the function, separated with commas. The code of the function must be enclosed within curly braces.

Following is what the code to emulate the built-in `sqrt()` function might look like, based on the fact that the square root of a number can be calculated by raising that number to the power of 0.5 – with the `pow()` function serving to calculate the power:

```
function SquareRoot($n)

{

   return pow($n, 0.5)

}
```

In this example the function created is `SquareRoot()`, and it accepts one argument (the value passed in the variable `$n`).

The function code comprises a single statement that simply calls the in-built `pow()` function, which accepts two values: a number and a value by which power the number should be raised. So the two values passed to it are n and 0.5.

The `return` Keyword

The function then calculates the square root and returns it, at which point the `return` keyword causes that value to be returned. It is then a simple matter of calling the function in the following manner to display a square root in the browser.

```
echo SquareRoot(49);
```

Or the value returned can be used in an expression, assigned to a variable, or used in numerous other ways.

Note: Of course, this code slightly cheats since it calls another in-built function called `pow()` (in which case we might as well simply call the in-built `sqrt()` function in the first place), but it serves to illustrate how to write a simple function that takes one value, and returns another after processing it.

Passing Arguments

In the preceding example you saw how to pass a single argument to a function, but you can pass as many as you need (or none), as shown with the following function that provides functionality that is not native to PHP (but is in some other languages), namely the ability to create a string by repeating a supplied string a set number of times.

For example, here's one way to recreate the PHP `str_repeat()` function:

```
function StrRepeat($s, $r)
{
  return implode($s, array_fill(0, ++$r, ''));
}
```

This function uses the sneaky trick of creating a new array using the `array_fill()` function that has the number of elements in the value `$r`, plus 1. So if `$r` has the value 3, then the new array is given four elements by pre-incrementing the value in `$r`. Each element is give the value ` ' '`, the empty string.

With the array now created, the `implode()` function is called in the outside expression. As you will recall from Lecture 7, `implode()` concatenates all the elements in an array into a string, placing the separator string in the value passed to `implode()` between each element value.

So if `$r` has the value 3, a four element array is created (with each element being empty). Then the `implode()` function concatenates these four elements together, placing the string in the variable `$s` between each occurrence. Therefore, since the array elements are empty, this entire statement will simply create three copies of the string in `$s` concatenated together, and that is the string that is returned from the function using the `return` keyword. Neat huh?

Accessing Arguments

Arguments received by a function are given the names you supply between the brackets. These do not need to be (and probably will mostly not be) the same as the variables or values passed to the function.

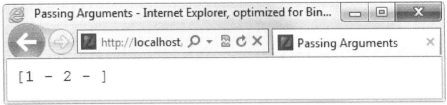

Figure 1: No third argument has been passed to the function.

Variables are assigned to the values received by a function in the order in which they are listed, and there can be as many or as few arguments as you like. Generally the number of arguments supplied to a function should be the same as the number the function expects to receive, but not always.

If a function receives fewer arguments than it is expecting it will assign the empty string to the remaining values, as shown in the following example (see Figure 10-1) in which the third argument has not been passed:

```
Example(1, 2);


function Example($a, $b, $c)
{
   echo "[$a - $b - $c]";
}
```

If your function sometimes uses the missing values and sometimes doesn't, this can cause an obscure and hard to track down bug. But there are times when you may not want to provide all the arguments to a function, because they may be optional.

For example, consider the in-built PHP function `implode()` which joins the elements of an array together into a string. Fort its first argument it accepts either no value, or a string value that will be used as the divider between each array element. If no separator argument is supplied then `implode()` assumes there will be no separator.

But, for example, you can write a new version of `implode()` to work in the same way as the similar JavaScript `join()` function, such that when no separator is specified then a comma will be assumed as the separator:

```
function NewImplode($arg1, $arg2)
{
   if (!isset($arg2)) return implode(',', $arg1);
   return implode($arg1, $arg2);
}
```

The key code that provides a default value works like this:

```
if (!isset($arg2)) return implode(',', $arg1);
```

This uses the PHP `isset()` function which returns TRUE if a variable exists or FALSE if it doesn't. So, if `$arg2` has no value, then only one argument was passed, which must be the array to implode. Therefore the array is imploded using the `implode()` function, with a comma passed as the separator.

On the other hand, if `$arg2` has a value, then `$arg1` is a separator value, so both `$arg1` and `$arg2` are passed to `implode()`. In either instance the `return` keyword returns the result of calling `implode()`.

Handling Unknown Numbers of Arguments

Rather than passing and accepting a known number of arguments, you can also access an unknown number of arguments by calling the `func_num_args()` function. This returns he number of arguments that have been passed to a function. Using this value and the `func_get_arg()` function, which retrieves a single argument, you can access all the arguments passed to a function as if it were an array using an index (from 0 to the number of elements minus 1).

To illustrate this lets emulate the `array()` function which itself supports any number of arguments passed to it, which it then places in an array which is returned, like this:

```
function NewArray()
{
   $n = func_num_args();
   $a = array();
```

```
    for($j = 0 ; $j < $n ; ++$j)
      array_push($a, func_get_arg($j));


    return $a;
  }
```

This function first looks up the number of arguments that have been passed to it and saves that value in $n. Then it creates a new array called $a. After that it iterates through all the arguments passed to the function, using $j as an index into the list. Each time around the loop the argument indicated is pushed onto the $a array. When the loop has completed the array $a is returned.

It is now possible to call this new function in place of array(), like this, for example:

```
    $Flowers = NewArray('Daisy', 'Lilly', 'Crocus');
```

Here the array $Flowers is created and populated with three elements. To verify that this is the case the following loop displays all these elements:

```
    foreach($Flowers as $flower) echo "$flower<br />";
```

Note: *The archive of example files at the companion website includes* arguments1.php, arguments2.php *and* arguments3.php, *which illustrate all the preceding discussions of argument passing and handling.*

Passing by Reference

In PHP, the & symbol, when prefaced to a variable, tells the parser to pass a reference to the variable's value, not the value itself. Normally, you see, when you pass an argument to a function only the value that the variable being passed contains is provided to the function. The original variable is untouched, and the function being called cannot change that variable's value.

However, when you pass a value by reference you give full access to the variable that contains that value to the called function, which is then able to modify the variable's contents if required to do so.

To pass a value by reference (rather than as a value extracted from a variable or array, for example), you simply place the & character before the variable name in the function call's argument list. For example, to change a string to lower case you would normally use a statement such as this:

```
$MyString = strtolower($MyString);
```

But you can also write your own function that will do the job without you having to type the string name in twice, and that function might look like this:

```
function ToLower(&$v)
{
  $v = strtolower($v);
}
```

Now you can set $MyString to lower case with less effort, like this:

```
ToLower(&$MyString);
```

What will happen is that due to the & preceding it, $MyString is passed by reference to ToLower() (rather than just sending the value stored in $MyString). ToLower() then modifies the variable passed to it, which means the original variable's value is updated.

Global and Local Variable Scope

Up to this point I have left out a very important keyword which you will certainly have seen if you have viewed the source of any PHP code, and that's the global keyword. After introducing it here, you'll see me using it a lot more. However, I left out its inclusion until now because I didn't want to get you bogged down by the difference between *local* and *global* variables. But you are ready for it now!

So far I have treated all the variables created in the course as having local scope (except when passing a value to a function by reference). This means that once defined you can access their values and modify them from the current part of the program, which is either of the following:

• If created outside of a function, the scope covers all code that resides outside of function calls, as well as those in included files.

- If created within a function, the scope covers that function only.

Using Local Variables

Therefore, so far in this course I have used only local variables. Let me illustrate this to you with some code:

```
$MyVar = 1;
echo 'Outside: $MyVar == ' .$MyVar;


Example();


function Example()
{
   echo 'Inside: $MyVar == ' . "$MyVar<br />";
}
```

In this example the variable $MyVar is created in the main part of the program (outside of any functions), and is assigned the value 1. Then the variable's value is displayed, and if you run the code you will see the value 1 is output.

But then the function Example() is called, which also displays the value in $MyVar, and when this code is run nothing is output. The reason for this is that $MyVar has only local scope (which is the default), and therefore it can be read from and written to only outside of any functions (and also in any included code that is also outside of any functions).

In order to give the Example() function access to the variable it must define it as being global using the following statement:

```
global $MyVar;
```

Therefore, the following updated version of the previous example will now display the value of 1 both outside and inside the function:

```
$MyVar = 1;
echo 'Outside: $MyVar == ' . "$MyVar<br />";
```

```
Example();

function Example()
{
  global $MyVar;
  echo 'Inside: $MyVar == ' . $MyVar;
}
```

Even though you can do so, there is no point using the global keyword outside of a function because it will not make that variable referenced by it available to any functions. Only by using the global keyword from inside a function will access be granted to that variable.

You can make more than one variable have global scope within a function by separating their names with commas, like this:

```
global $MyVar, $ThisVar, $ThatVar;
```

You may not, however, try to assign a value to a variable from a global statement, as in the following example, which is invalid syntax and will not work since you may only list variable (or array etc) names after the global keyword:

```
global $MyVar = 2; // This is not a valid statement
```

The correct alternative is to use two statements, like this:

```
global $MyVar;
$MyVar = 2;
```

The following code illustrates more clearly the difference between local and global scope:

```
$MyVar1 = 1;
$MyVar2 = 2;
```

```
echo 'Outside of any functions<br /><br />';
echo '$MyVar1 = ' . "$MyVar1<br />";
echo '$MyVar2 = ' . "$MyVar2<br /><br />";


Example();


function Example()
{
   global $MyVar2;

   echo 'Inside a function<br /><br />';
   echo '$MyVar1 = ' . "$MyVar1<br />";
   echo '$MyVar2 = ' . $MyVar2;
}
```

Here $MyVar1$ is give a value of 1 and $MyVar2$ a value of 2. Both these assignments occur outside of any functions, and the echo statements verify these assignments have been successfully made.

Then Example() is called and the code in this function only gives $MyVar2$ global scope, so when the value of $MyVar1$ is displayed nothing is output since, as far as the function is concerned, that variable doesn't exist. However, since it has global scope the value in $MyVar2$ is displayed.

Figure 10-2 shows the result of running this code (available as *local.php* in the companion archive) in a browser.

What this means is that all variable names are free for re-use inside all functions so that, for example, you could reuse the variable $count many times over in different functions, without any use conflicting with any other use.

This is the case because when a function returns it also forgets all the local variables that have been used in it. However, any changes the function makes to any variables it has given global scope to remain in place when the function returns.

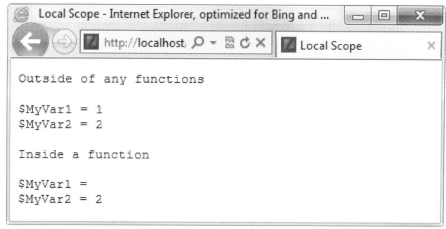

Figure 2: Only $MyVar2$ *is global so* $MyVar1$ *has no value in the function.*

The use of the `global` keyword in PHP is not the same as in some other programming languages, because what the keyword really means in PHP is "Give this function access to the variable's value", it does not make a variable fully global to all code in a program. Therefore, even though the `global` keyword may be applied to a variable with one function, that same variable will *not* have global scope in any other functions, unless they too use the `global` keyword to gain access to it.

The $GLOBALS[] Array

Normally in PHP you can manage almost every programming task using local variables, with occasional use of giving a function global access to the odd variable. It also makes for clear and more bug-free code to avoid extensive use of global variables.

However, there are occasions when you find no simpler way to manage a particular task, and for these times PHP provides you with the `$GLOBALS[]` array. This is a pre-defined array that has full global scope both outside and inside functions, and with the requirement to use the `global` keyword.

To save a value with global access you place it in the `$GLOBALS[]` array, like this:

```
echo $GLOBALS["MyVar"];
```

Therefore, even though no `global` keyword has been used, as long as `$MyVar` was created outside of any functions (or within the current function) it can be accessed.

Although if it's created in the current function it cannot be accessed elsewhere globally by any means whatsoever.

Let's look at a slightly modified version of the `Example()` function in the previous example, which will now display all variable's values, with the difference highlighted in bold:

```php
function Example()
{
  global $MyVar2;

  echo 'Inside a function<br /><br />';
  echo '$MyVar1 == ' . $GLOBALS["MyVar1"] . '<br />';
  echo '$MyVar2 == ' . $MyVar2;
}
```

Now, the value in `$MyVar1` is correctly output because it has been looked up using the `$GLOBALS[]` array. The file *global.php* in the companion archive contains this updated code.

You can also write a value back to a global variable using `$GLOBALS[]` like this:

```php
$GLOBALS["MyVar1"] = 3;
```

The main benefit of using the `$GLOBALS[]` array is that it is immediately obvious to yourself (or any other programmer who updates your code) that you are accessing a global variable. On the other hand, after using the `global` keyword, it is not immediately apparent that a variable has global scope.

Note: Remember that when accessing a global variable via the $GLOBALS[] array you must omit the preceding $ and place the remainder of the variable name inside quotes.

Global Naming Convention

I write a lot of PHP code and found that for each variable used I would still have to keep referring back to see whether it had a `global` keyword applied at any point in a function (making it global), or if no `global` keyword was used it would then be local. To save me from having to keep rechecking I came up with the following simple convention.

Whenever a variable is created that requires global scope I use all uppercase letters, and when a local variable is created I use lower case, or a combination of upper and lower case, like this:

```
$HIGHSCORE  = 0    // Creates a global variable
$HighScore += 100 // Increments a local variable
```

Therefore any variables I use that have any lowercase letters I can be sure are being used as local variables, and where it's required I also ensure I use the `global` keyword on a variable's first use in a function.

Of course, you can use any other convention you like (such as prefacing global variables with `G_`), or no convention at all.

Summary

Congratulations. With the use of functions under your belt you can now call yourself a PHP programmer. However, there are still a few more steps to take before you can call yourself a master of the language – starting in the following lecture with PHP objects, which enable you to write OOP (Object Oriented Programming).

PHP
OBJECTS

By following this lecture you will:

- ✓ *Understand the principles of Object Oriented Programming.*
- ✓ *Know how to create object classes.*
- ✓ *Be able to create instances of classes and use them.*

PHP IS SO much more than simply a scripting language because it also offers the power and flexibility of object oriented programming (OOP). This is a style of programming in which the data used by a program and the code to manipulate it are all provided together in bundles called objects.

For example, a standard (or procedural) programming language will treat data and code as two separate entities, although some steps towards using objects are made in terms of providing access to functions. Indeed, enabling the use of local variables in functions also takes a further step towards modularity. But that's about as far as a non-OOP language generally goes.

On the other hand, a language that embraces OOP encourages you to place data where it is not directly accessible by the rest of the program. Instead, the data is accessed by calling specially written functions (commonly called methods) which are either bundled in with the data or inherited from class objects.

An object-oriented program will usually contain different types of objects, with each type corresponding to a particular kind of complex data to be managed, or a real-world object or concept such as a car, football team or dental practice.

For example, in the case of providing social networking facility to a website, there may be a number of objects to program, such as one for signing up new users, another for users to manage their accounts, another to enable messaging between accounts, and so on.

OOP Terminology

There are a number of terms you need to get used to when you first start to program using OOP. To start with the combination of code and the data it manipulates is called a *class*. Each new object created that is based on a class is called an *instance* of that class (also known as an *occurrence*).

Within a class the data associated with it are called its *properties*, while the functions it uses to access that data are called its *methods*. Whenever you see the term method used in relation to programming, it's simply another word for function, but it implies that OOP programming is being discussed.

The objective of OOP is to write methods in such a way that only they can access their associated properties. This is known as *encapsulation*, and the idea is to prevent tainting of data by preventing any functions other than the methods of a class from manipulating its properties. The methods you build into a class are known as the *interface*.

Classes may contain a method used to initialize an instance of the class, and this type of method is called a *constructor*.

The reason OOP can be much safer than procedural programming is that, due to encapsulation, only the methods in a certain class can access its properties. Therefore there is only one place to go when you need to debug your code – the methods of a class. You will not need to look anywhere else in your code to solve a bug relating to how the properties of a class are manipulated.

Other benefits are that once you have created and debugged a class, you may find you later need another one that is similar. Whenever that happens you can save yourself a tremendous amount of development time by simply defining a new class based on the existing one. This is called *inheritance*, with the original class then becoming a *superclass*, while the new one is a *subclass* (also known as a *derived* class). This new subclass can then add its own properties and methods, as required.

Declaring a Class

The first step in object oriented programming is declaring a class, which defines a new type of object, but doesn't actually create the object. Classes group together a combination of data and the program code required to manipulate the data, into a single object.

To declare a class you use the `class` keyword, like this:

```
class UserClass
{
  public $firstname, $lastname;

  function GetName()
  {
    return $this->firstname . ' ' . $this->lastname;
  }
}
```

This creates the new class `UserClass` and gives it two items of data it can hold: `$firstname`, and `$lastname`. It also sets up a method (another name for a function) that can be applied to the class called `GetName()`, which returns a string with `$firstname` and `$lastname` concatenated together, separated with a space character.

The `$this` keyword refers to the current object and the `->` operator refers to a property of that object. It can also refer to a method of an object as well.

Creating an Object

You can now create a new object (known as an *instance*) based on this class, as follows (in which the new object `User` is created):

```
$User = new UserClass;
```

This creates the new object `$User`, which has all the properties and methods defined in the class. The object doesn't (yet) have any data in it, though.

Accessing Properties and Objects

Once an instance of a class has been created using the `new` keyword, you can populate the object with data like this:

```
$User->firstname = 'Julie';
$User->lastname  = 'Smith';
```

Once the object has some properties defined you can view them by calling the `GetName()` method, like this:

```
echo $User->GetName();
```

This will display the string "Julie Smith".

Note: *When referencing properties after the* `->` *operator, you must omit the preceding* `$` *symbol.*

Using a Constructor

To enable you to create a new object and populate it with data all at the same time you can create a constructor method in one of two ways. The first is to repeat the class name as a class method, like this (with the constructor method shown in bold):

```
class UserClass
{
  public $firstname, $lastname;

  function UserClass($firstname, $lastname)
  {
    $this->firstname = $firstname;
    $this->lastname  = $lastname;
  }

  function GetName()
```

```
    {
        return $this->firstname . ' ' . $this->lastname;
    }
}
```

Now you can pre-populate the object (in the same manner as pre-populating a new array) when you create the instance of the class, like this:

```
$User = new UserClass('Julie', 'Smith');
```

However there is a better way that is recommended to use instead of the preceding constructor, which is to use a method called __construct() as your constructor (two underscores followed by the word construct), like this:

```
function __construct($firstname, $lastname)
{
    $this->firstname = $firstname;
    $this->lastname  = $lastname;
}
```

Note: It is always recommended to use a constructor method to ensure encapsulation. Without one data properties must be separately assigned, and it may be tempting to do so by directly manipulating the property values of an object (for example, by the statement $User->lastname = 'Jones';). However, if you require the initial values to be assigned to an object's properties when the object is first created you avoid this. To maintain full encapsulation, you should also write methods for the object's class that will update the properties in future, rather than directly updating them.

Destructors

You can also provide a destructor method to be called when the code has need the final reference to an object, or when a script reaches the end. To create one use code such as this (where the method name is two underscores followed by the word destruct):

```
function __destruct()
{
```

```
    // Place your destructor code here
}
```

Object Cloning

After creating an object it will be passed by reference when passed as a parameter. This means that when assigning a new object based on an existing one you don't actually copy the old object to the new one – you simply create a reference to the existing object. Therefore the following code does not create a copy of $OldObject:

```
$NewObject = $OldObject; // Creates a reference to $OldObject
```

All that has happened here is that both $NewObject and $OldObject now refer to the same object. This is important to remember because it can result in unexpected bugs for beginners to OOP.

If you actually do want to create a new (and totally independent object) from an existing one, then you must use the clone keyword, like this:

```
$NewObject = clone $OldObject; // Creates a copy of $OldObject
```

This creates a brand new instance of the object with its own methods and properties, and which is completely unconnected to the original object. The way it works is to create a new instance of the class used by the original object, then it copies all the properties from the old object to the new one.

Static Methods and Properties

Sometimes you want to be able to supply a method that is called on a class and not on an instance of the class (an object). This type of method is suitable where you wish to perform an action that relates to the class and not to any particular instance. For example, you might need a method to ask users for their first and last names so that you can create a new object. This method will apply to the class but not to the objects, so you would write it like this (placing it inside the class definition):

```
Static function EnterName()
{
```

```
    // Display a form with input fields etc
  }
```

Static methods are called differently from regular ones, in that you don't use the `->` operator. Instead you use a double colon operator (known as the *scope resolution* operator), like this (assuming that `EnterName()` is a method of the class `UserClass`):

```
  UserClass::EnterName();
```

Or, from within another method of the class, you can refer to the static method like this:

```
  self::EnterName();
```

This saves on memory because this static method is only part of the class, and is not copied to all instances of the class, since doing so is unnecessary and wasteful.

Likewise you can create static properties that relate only to the class and not to any specific instances. For example, you may wish to track the number of users you have and the place to store that figure would be in a static property, like this:

```
  static $UserCount;
```

From within a method of a class you could then refer to this property with the `self` keyword and scope resolution operator, like this:

```
  self::$UserCount = 47362;
```

Or from outside the class you could access it like this (assuming the class it is attached to is `UserClass`):

```
  echo UserClass::UserCount;
```

Pre-defined Properties

When declaring properties in a class you may supply default values that will be used if none are supplied, like this:

```
  function __construct($firstname = 'anonymous', $lastname = 'user')
```

If values are supplied to the constructor, these default values will be ignored and the supplied ones will be applied.

OOP Constants

PHP supports the creation of constants in classes but you use a different syntax from the standard `define()` function for regular constants. Instead you use the `const` keyword, like this:

```
Class UserClass
{
  const VERSION = 1.21;

  function DispVer()
  {
    echo self::VERSION;
  }
}
```

For a method within a class, the constant's value is returned by applying the `self` keyword, followed by the scope resolution operator (`::`) and the constant's name. Or you can access it directly, like this:

```
echo UserClass::VERSION;
```

Like regular constants, once defined they cannot be changed.

Property and Method Scope

So far all the properties and methods in this lecture have been `public`, so that they have been fully accessible, even to the point of directly assigning values to object properties. However, this is not considered good OOP practice because it breaks the encapsulation.

Therefore PHP provides a means for you to restrict access to properties and methods in different ways using three keywords:

- `public` These properties are the default when declaring a variable using the `var` or `public` keywords, or when a variable is implicitly declared the first time it is used. The keywords `var` and `public` are interchangeable, because, although deprecated, var is retained for compatibility with previous versions of PHP. Methods are assumed to be `public` by default.
- `protected` These properties and methods (members) can be referenced only by the object's class methods and those of any subclasses.
- `private` These members can be referenced only by methods within the same class – not by subclasses.

Here's how to decide which you need to use:

- Use `public` when outside code should access this member and extending classes should also inherit it.
- Use `protected` when outside code should not access this member but extending classes should inherit it.
- Use `private` when outside code should not access this member and extending classes also should not inherit it.

The following example illustrates these keywords in use:

```
class Example
{
   var        $firstname;    // As public but deprecated
   public     $lastname;     // A public property
   protected  $age;          // A protected property

   private function Admin() // A private method
   {
      // Code for administration goes here
   }
}
```

In most cases, for proper encapsulation, you should probably set your properties and methods to `protected`. That way you'll keep your objects as self-contained as possible.

Applying Inheritance

When you've written a good class that you'd like to use elsewhere you can use the `extends` keyword when building a new class to incorporate all the features of the existing one. So, for example, assume you have the following class:

```php
class UserClass
{
  public $firstname, $lastname;

  function UserClass($firstname, $lastname)
  {
    $this->firstname = $firstname;
    $this->lastname  = $lastname;
  }

  function GetName()
  {
    return $this->firstname . ' ' . $this->lastname;
  }
}
```

Now, let's say you want to create a new class that will deal with a firstname and lastname, and which also handles usernames and passwords. To do so, all you need to add is the following, for example:

```php
class Subscriber extends UserClass
{
  public $username, $password;

  function ShowDetails()
  {
    echo "Firstname: "  . $this->firstname . '<br />';
```

```
      echo "Lastname :   " . $this->lastname  . '<br />';

      echo "Username :   " . $this->username  . '<br />';

      echo "Password :   " . $this->password  . '<br />';

   }

}
```

The new class `Subscriber` now embodies all the properties and methods of both classes, as can be verified by issuing the following statements:

```
$User             = new Subscriber('Julie', 'Smith');

$User->username = 'jsmith01';

$User->password = 'letmein';

echo $User->ShowDetails();
```

This results in the following being displayed:

Firstname: Julie
Lastname : Smith
Username : jsmith01
Password : letmein

Using the `parent` Operator

If you write a method in a subclass with the same name of one in its parent class, its statements will override those of the parent class. Sometimes this is not the behavior you want and you need to access the parent's method. To do this, you can use the `parent` operator, as demonstrated by the following example:

```
$object = new Child;
$object->output1();
$object->output2();

class Father
{
  function output1()
  {
    echo "[Class Father] I am your Father<br />";
```

```
      }
   }

   class Child extends Father
   {
     function output1()
     {
       echo "[Class Child] I am Luke<br />";
     }

     function output2()
     {
       parent::output1();

     }
   }
```

This code creates a class called `Father` and then a subclass called `Child` that inherits its properties and methods, then overrides the method `output1()`. Therefore, when line 2 calls the method `output1()`, the new method is executed. The only way to execute the overridden `output1()` method in the `Father` class is to use the `parent` operator, as shown in function `output2()` of class `Child`. The code outputs the following:

> [Class Child] I am Luke
> [Class Father] I am your Father

If you wish to ensure that your code calls a method from the current class, you can use the `self` keyword, like this:

```
   self::method();
```

Writing Subclass Constructors

When you extend a class and declare your own constructor, PHP will not automatically call the constructor method of the parent class. To be certain that all initialization code is executed, subclasses should always call the parent constructors, like this:

```
   $object = new ChocChip();
   echo "Choc Chip Cookies have these properties...\n";
   echo 'Chewy    : ' . $object->chewy . "\n";
   echo 'Chocolate : ' . $object->chocolate;
```

```
class Cookie
{
  public $chewy; // Cookies are chewy

  function __construct()
  {
    $this->chewy = 'TRUE';
  }
}

class ChocChip extends Cookie
{
  public $chocolate; // Choc Chip cookies have chocolate

  function __construct()
  {
    parent::__construct(); // Call parent constructor first
    $this->chocolate = 'TRUE';
  }
}
```

In this example the Cookie class has created the property $chewy, which is re-used in the ChocChip class, which inherits it. Additionally the ChocChip class creates another property, $chocolate.

Note how the ChocChip subclass constructor calls its parent class constructor using the parent keyword and the scope resolution operator (::).

The output from this code is as follows:

```
Choc Chip Cookies have these properties...
Chewy    : TRUE
Chocolate: TRUE
```

Using final Methods

Sometimes you may wish to prevent a method from being overwritten by a subclass and you can do this using the final keyword, like this:

```
final function Author()
{
    echo 'Written by Fred Bloggs';
}
```

When you use code such as this the function will be inherited by all subclasses and cannot be overwritten by a method of the same name. You cannot, however, use the `final` keyword on properties. Instead you should probably think about using a constant.

Summary

You are now becoming a power PHP programmer, capable of bending the will of the language itself to your desire. All that remains to finish your training (before moving onto using PHP in meaningful ways in your web pages) is to flesh your knowledge out a bit by looking at things such as how to gracefully handle errors in your code, and how to use regular expressions for powerful pattern matching – both of which are in the following lecture.

ERRORS AND EXPRESSIONS

By following this lecture you will:

- ✓ *Learn how to trap and handle errors.*
- ✓ *Use regular expressions for pattern matching.*
- ✓ *Be able to search and replace complex strings.*

THERE'S NO GETTING away from it, even the most careful programmers build unexpected errors (or bugs) into their code, and so will you – it's perfectly normal. And even after you think you've fully debugged your code the likelihood remains that there may still be obscure bugs lurking somewhere.

The last thing you want on a published website is for users to encounter errors, or sometimes even worse, just find your code doesn't work for them – making them leave to never return.

But PHP comes with ways you can minimize the problem by attaching your own function to the standard error trapping routines.

In this lecture I'll show you how you can manipulate PHP's in-built error trapping for dealing with bugs, and also how you can use regular expressions to perform powerful and complex pattern matching in simple statements.

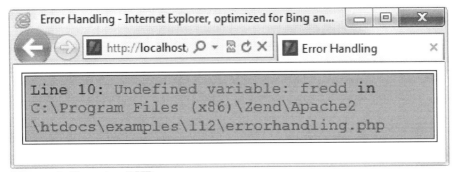

Figure 1: Trapping PHP errors.

Error Trapping

Although you can't catch fatal errors (such as typing `echho` instead of `echo`) in PHP, it is possible to trap runtime errors in your code by adding the following statement and function to the start of any PHP program:

```
set_error_handler("ErrorHandler");

function ErrorHandler($no, $str, $file, $line)
{
    echo "<table border='1' cellpadding='5'><tr><td bgcolor='tan'>" .
        "Line $line: <font color='red'>$str</font> in " .
        "<font color='blue'>$file</font></td></tr></table>";
}
```

Then, whenever a runtime error occurs, such as from the following typographical error, a message such that shown in Figure 12-1 will be displayed:

```
$fred = 1;
echo $fredd;
```

This makes it far quicker to catch and correct obscure errors you may introduce into your code and is achieved simply by pointing PHP's standard error trapping code to a new function that replaces it. If you want to restore PHP's own error handling at some point in your code, just add the following statement:

```
restore_error_handler();
```

You can get copy and paste this code from the file *errorhandling.php* in the archive of examples on the companion website. Just remember to remove the error trapping code when you move it to a production website after all bugs have been corrected.

Regular Expressions

Regular expressions were invented as a means of matching an enormous variety of different types of pattern with just a single expression. Using them you can replace several lines of code with a simple expression, and can even use regular expressions in replace as well as search operations.

To properly learn everything there is to know about regular expressions could take a whole book (and, indeed, books have been written on the subject), so I'm just going to introduce you to the basics in this lecture, but if you need to know more I recommend you check out the following URL as a good starting point:

```
wikipedia.org/wiki/Regular_expression
```

In PHP you will use regular expressions mostly in two functions: `preg_match()` and `preg_replace()`. The `preg_match()` function tells you whether its argument matches the regular expression, while `preg_replace()` takes a second parameter: the string to replace the text that matches.

Using `preg_match()`

Let's say you want to find out whether one string occurs within another. For example, if you wish to know if the string `'whether'` occurs in Hamlet's famous soliloquy you might use code such as the following:

```
$s = "To be, or not to be, that is the question: "   .
      "Whether 'tis Nobler in the mind to suffer"     .
```

```
        "The Slings and Arrows of outrageous Fortune, " .
        "Or to take Arms against a Sea of troubles, "   .
        "And by opposing end them.";


    $r = '/whether/';
    $n = preg_match($r, $s, $match);
    echo "$r matches: $match[0]";
```

In this example the variable $r is a regular expression object that is given the value '/whether/', which is how you denote a regular expression. First you place a / character, then the text to match, followed by a closing / character. In this example, however, a match is not made because (by default) regular expressions are case-sensitive, and only the word Whether (with an upper case W) exists in the string.

If you wish to make a case-insensitive search you can tell PHP by placing the letter i after the closing / character, like this (in this case a match will be made):

```
    $r = '/whether/i';
```

You don't have to place a regular expression in an object first if you choose not to, so two lines can be replaced with the following single statement:

```
    $n = preg_match('/whether/i', $s, $match);
```

The result of executing these statements results in $match[0] containing the match if there was one. The variable $match[] is an array, so that it is able to store more than a single value, even though this particular statement only looks for only a single match. When it returns preg_match() returns a value of 1 if there was a match, 0 if none was found, or -1 if an error occurred.

If all you are doing is testing whether one string appears in another you may prefer to use strpos() or strstr() instead as they will be much quicker. For more details on preg_match() please see this page:

```
    php.net/manual/en/function.preg-match.php
```

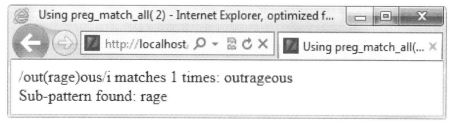

Figure 2: The main pattern and sub-pattern have been found.

Using `preg_match_all()`

The preceding code is great for when you need to see whether there's at least a single instance of a search word in a target string, but when you want to find out how many matches there are you need to use the `preg_match_all()` function, like this:

```php
$n = preg_match_all('/to/i', $s, $match);
echo "$r matches " . sizeof($match[0]) . ' times: ';
echo join(', ', $match[0]);
```

In this example the word 'to' is being searched for in a case-insensitive manner. The matches are returned into the array `$match[0]` so the `sizeof()` function is used to display how many matches there were. Then the `join()` function (an alias of `implode()`) displays all occurrences separated with commas. The array `$match[]` now contains a sub-array in `$match[0]` containing all the matches found.

The contents of `$match[1]` and other elements will contain text that matched the first captured parenthesized sub-pattern (if any). For example, when pattern matching you may place sub patterns within round brackets, and when they are matched they will appear in these elements of `$match[]`, like this:

```php
$r = '/out(rage)ous/i';
$n = preg_match_all($r, $s, $match);
echo "$r matches " . sizeof($match[0]) . ' times: ';
echo join(', ', $match[0]);
echo '<br />Sub-pattern found: ' . $match[1][0];
```

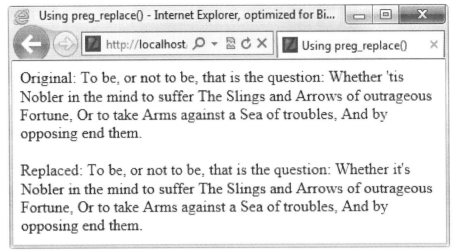

Figure 3: Applying `preg_replace()` *(see the top-right of each phrase).*

Here the word 'rage' is placed in brackets within the search pattern in $r. When this code is run the 'rage' sub-pattern is found and is placed in the first element of a sub-array of $match[1], as shown in Figure 12-2.

Using `preg_replace()`

You can also replace matched text using the `preg_replace()` function. The source string is not modified by this because `preg_replace()` returns a new string with all the changes made.

So, for example, to replace the string `'tis` in the soliloquy with the word `it's` (although Shakespeare would surely object), you could use a regular expression and the `preg_replace()` function like this:

```
preg_replace("/'tis/", "it's", $r);
```

Figure 12-3 shows the result of executing this statement (using the file *preg_replace.htm* in the accompanying archive). In it you can see that the word after `Whether` is now `it's`.

As with `preg_match()` you can specify a case-insensitive replace by placing an `i` character at the end of the regular expression, as in the following example :

```
preg_replace("/'tis/i", "it's", $r);
```

Unlike `preg_match()` the `preg_replace()` function will automatically replace all matches it discovers. It's also more powerful in that the subject of the replace operation can be an array, in which case the replacement will occur on all strings in the array.

You may also provide an option fourth argument to the function, which will have the number of replacements made saved into it, like this:

```
preg_replace("/'tis/i", "it's", $r, $count);
```

Upon return `$count` will contain the number of replacements made.

Fuzzy Matching

Regular expressions are a lot more powerful than simply searching for and replacing words and phrases, because they also support complex fuzzy logic features through the use of *metacharacters*.

There are several types of metacharacter but let's look at just one for now, the * character, to see how they work. When you place a * in a regular expression it is not treated as that asterisk character, but as a metacharacter with a special meaning, which is that when performing a match the character immediately preceding the * may appear in the searched string any number of times (or not at all).

This type of metacharacter is particularly useful for sweeping up lots of blank space so that you can, for example, search for any of the strings `'back pack'`, `'backpack'`, `'back  pack'` (with two spaces between the words), `'Back Pack'` (with mixed case), and many other combinations, like this:

```
$s = "Have you seen my BackPack anywhere?";
preg_match('/back *pack/i', $s, $match);
```

Because the `i` character is also used the matching is case-insensitive, and so the word `BackPack` is found by the regular expression, and the `echo` command displays the result in the browser. You can try this for yourself using the file *fuzzy.php* in the archive file available at the companion website.

Metacharacters	Action
/	Begins and ends a regular expression
.	Matches any character other than newline
*	Matches previous element zero or more times
+	Matches previous element one or more times
?	Matches previous element zero or one time
[characters]	Matches a single character out of those contained within the brackets
[^characters]	Matches a single character that is not contained within the brackets
(regexp)	Treats regexp as a group for counting, or following *, + or ?
left|right	Matches either left or right
l–r	(Within square brackets) Matches a range of characters between l and r
^	(Outside of square brackets) Requires the match to be at the search string's start
$	(Outside of square brackets) Requires the match to be at the search string's end

Table 12-1: The basic metacharacters.

Note: *If you want to use any of the characters that are metacharacters as regular characters in your regular expressions you must escape them by preceding the characters with a \ character. For example * will turn the * from a metacharacter into a simple asterisk.*

Matching Any Character

You can get even fuzzier than that, though, with the period (or dot) character, which can stand in for any character at all (except a newline). For example to find all

Other	Action
\b	Matches a word boundary
\B	Matches where there isn't a word boundary
\d	Matches a digit
\D	Matches a non-digit
\n	Matches a newline character
\s	Matches a whitespace character
\S	Matches a non-whitespace character
\t	Matches a tab character
\w	Matches one of a-z, A-Z, 0-9 or _
\W	Matches any character but a-z, A-Z, 0-9 or _
\x	(Where x is a metacharacter) Treats x as a normal character
{n}	Matches exactly n times
{n,}	Matches n times or more
{min, max}	Matches at least min and at most max times

Table 12-2: Escape and numeric range metacharacters.

HTML tags (which start with < and end with >) you could use the following regular expression (in any of a `preg_match()`, `preg_match_all()` or `preg_replace()` call:

```
"/<.*>/"
```

The left and right angle brackets either side serve as the start and end points for each match. Within them this expression will match any character due to the dot metacharacter, while the * after the dot says there can be zero, one or any number of these characters. Therefore any size of HTML tag, from the meaningless <> upwards will be matched.

Example	Matches
`\.`	The first . in *Hello there. Nice to see you.*
`h`	The first h in *My hovercraft is full of eels*
`lemon`	The word *lemon* in *I like oranges and lemons*
`orange|lemon`	Either *orange* or *lemon* in I like oranges and lemons
`bel[ei][ei]ve`	Either *believe* or *beleive* (also *beleeve* or *beliive*)
`bel[ei]{2}ve`	Either *believe* or *beleive* (also *beleeve* or *beliive*)
`bel(ei)|(ie)ve`	Either *believe* or *beleive* (but not *beleeve* or *beliive*)
`2\.0*`	*2., 2.0, 2.00* and so on
`j-m`	Any of the characters *j, k, l,* or *m*
`house$`	Only the final *house* in *This house is my house*
`^can`	Only the first *can* in *can you open this can?*
`\d{1,2}`	And one or two digit number from *0* to *9* and *00* to *99*
`[\w]+`	Any word of at least one character
`[\w]{3}`	Any three letter word

Table 12-3: Some example regular expressions and their matches.

Other metacharacters include the + symbol, which works like the *, except that it will match one or more characters, so you could avoid matching <> by ensuring there is always at least one character between the angle brackets, like this:

```
"/<.+>/"
```

Unfortunately, because the * and + characters will match all the way up to the last > on a line, as well as catching single tags like <h1>Heading</h1>, they can also catch nested HTML such as <h1>Heading</h1>.

Not Matching a Character

A solution to the multi-tag matching problem is to use the ^ character whose meaning is 'anything but', but which must be placed within square brackets, like this:

```
" [^>]+"
```

This regular expression is like .+ except there is one character it refuses to match, the > symbol. Therefore, when presented with the string `<h1><i>Heading</i></h1>`, the expression will now stop at the first > encountered, and so the initial `<h1>` tag will be properly matched. Table 12-1 summarizes the basic metacharacters and their actions.

Some of the characters in Table 12-1 I have already explained, while some should be self-explanatory. Others, however you may find confusing, so I would recommend only using those you understand until you have learned more about regular expressions, perhaps from the Wikipedia article listed a little earlier, or from the comprehensive, multi-page tutorial at this URL:

```
tinyurl.com/phpregex
```

There is also a selection of escape metacharacters and numeric ranges you can include, listed in Table 12-2. To help you better understand how these various metacharacters can work together, in Table 12-3 I have detailed a selection of regular expression examples, and the matches they will make.

Remember that you can place the character i after the closing / of a regular expression to make it case-insensitive and can also place the character m after the final / to put the expression into multi-line mode, so that the ^ and $ characters will match at the start and end of any newlines in the string, rather than the default of the string's start and end.

Note: You may use any combination of the i, g and m modifiers after your regular expressions.

Summary

This lecture has covered some fairly advanced things, including error handling and sophisticated pattern matching, and it tops off the last items of basic knowledge you need about the PHP language. Starting with the following lecture I will, therefore, concentrate on how to use PHP to interact dynamically with users.

WEB FORMS AND SECURITY

By following this lecture you will:

- ✓ *Know how to process data posted to PHP from a form.*
- ✓ *Be able to write code to upload files to a server.*
- ✓ *Learn how to secure PHP from potential hacking.*

Even in these days of advanced Web 2.0 websites, with hyper-interactivity and self-updating pages using behinds the scenes communication with web servers via Ajax (detailed in Lecture 14), most websites still rely on trust HTML forms for requesting input from users.

HTML forms are simple, easily implemented and have passed the test of time. What's more they can be simply constructed in HTML or output from a scripting language such as PHP.

There is a downside, though, which is that even on a securely encrypted connection there's no guarantee that the data being sent from the user isn't going to be potentially malicious. And especially on non-encrypted links it's possible for hackers to construct copies of web forms either in HTML or created from software to send badly formed data to a web server, hoping to somehow gain entry to it or otherwise compromise the server.

Therefore this lecture focuses on how you can create effective forms that are easily processed via PHP, and also it points out potential security hazards and pitfalls, and show you how you can avoid them.

Creating a Form

Whether created in a simple HTML page, or assembled via output from a program such as PHP, all web forms must have the following:

- Opening and closing <form> and </form> tags.
- A submission method of either Post or Get.
- One or more input fields (although you can omit them, but you won't be able to send any data if you do).
- A destination URL of a program to receive the form data.

The following example illustrates how to build a very simple form to ask a user for their Username and Password from PHP. It is output using echo statements, but could equally have used print() calls or Heredocs:

```
<!DOCTYPE html>
<html>
  <head>
    <title>A Simple Form</title>
  </head>
  <body><pre>
<?php
    echo "<form method='post' action='simpleform.php'>";
    echo "Enter Username: <input type='text'     name='username' />\n";
    echo "Enter Password: <input type='password' name='password' />\n";
    echo "<input type='submit' /></form>";
?>
  </pre></body>
</html>
```

This code starts off by specifying the standard HTML5 !DOCTYPE and then displays some HTML, and in the middle there's a section of PHP code that displays the web form.

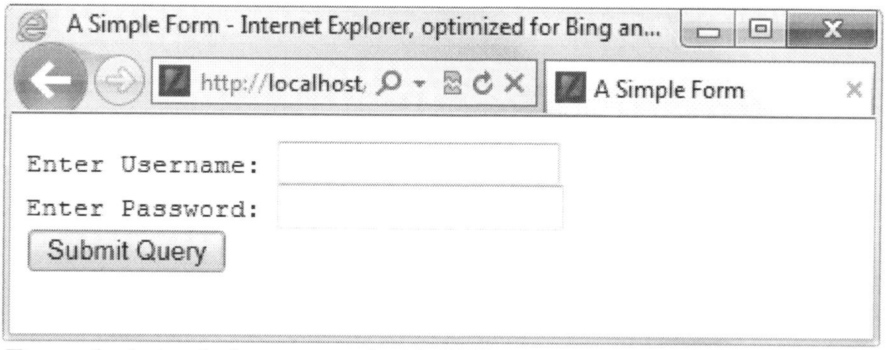

Figure 1: A simple form created with PHP.

This PHP opens a form and specifies a `method` of `get` for sending the data, and that the form data should post to the file named *simpleform.php*. If this example is saved using that filename then it will post to itself.

The type of data expected for the Username field is `text`, but that for the Password field is `password`. This has the effect of displaying only * characters when data is entered into this field, keeping it secure from any prying eyes.

When displayed in a browser the code looks like Figure 13-1. Note how I have used `<pre>` and `</pre>` tags for brevity to apply some simple formatting by ensuring the font used is monospaced, and that linefeeds are applied in the right places using the `\n` escape characters.

The Difference between Post and Get Requests

In this example the data is being sent using a Post request, which sends the information using headers so that they are not visible to the user. It could equally have used a Get method instead, but this would require the receiving program to retrieve the data slightly differently.

The reason is that Get request data is attached to the end of the URL that is being posted to in the form of a query string. This is a tail containing various information that you often see following regular URLs. When you search Google for the term PHP (for example), the results page will display a URL similar to the following in the address field:

```
http://www.google.com/search?q=PHP&ie=utf-8&oe=utf-8
```

In fact the URL will likely be longer than that, as I have retained only the first three items of data in the query string, as follows:

- q Has the value PHP
- ie Has the value utf
- oe Has the value utf-8

The query string starts with a ? character and is then followed by one or more pairs of field names and values. Each pair is separated by a & character, and the fields and values themselves are separated with an = character.

Security Issues With Get Requests

Since Post requests are sent using headers they are not revealed to the user, but because Get requests are appended to the URL being posted to, it is easy for the user any anyone else with access to that computer to see the query data by referring to the address field.

So if the data contains sensitive information such as a password, even though it has been displayed using * characters in the input field, it is out in plain view in the address field. More than that, if a page that was arrived at from a Get request is bookmarked then all that query data will be stored in the bookmark URL, which can be easily located by even the most casual of snoopers.

There's an additional security risk with Get requests in that most web server save the full URLs of all pages called up on a server in their log files. This means that should these logs get into the wrong hands, any sensitive data will be compromised.

Note: For these reasons I always recommend that you avoid using Get requests unless you have a compelling reason for doing so, and the data being transmitted is not of a sensitive nature.

Accessing The Form Data From PHP

It is possible for a PHP program to extract Get data from the query string directly, but it takes some fiddly code to separate out all the fields and values. However, whichever method is used to send form data to a PHP program, there's an easy way of accessing it, via either the $_GET[] or $_POST[] arrays, which will be pre-populated with the data by PHP.

For example, the following places the data posted from the preceding example into to variables:

```
$username = $_POST['username'];
$password = $_POST['password'];
```

And you can also obtain Get method data like this:

```
$username = $_GET['username'];
$password = $_GET['password'];
```

In fact it's possible to make your PHP programs accept either type of input with the following code:

```
$username = isset($_POST['username']) ?
  $_POST['username'] : $_GET['username'];
$password = isset($_POST['password']) ?
  $_POST['password'] : $_GET['password'];
```

Here the ? ternary operator is used to test whether the $_POST[] array contains the data by calling the isset() function. If it is then the data is read from there, otherwise it is read form the $_GET[] array.

About register_globals

In the early days of PHP there was a register_globals setting that could be applied and was on by default. When it was on then all form data sent to a PHP program was automatically saved in variables of the same name as the fields.

In the preceding example, therefore, regardless of whether a Get or Post method was used, $username and $password would automatically be created and given the values entered into the form. This was great and programmers thought it was a wonderful idea, until a few problems crept up.

It was soon discovered by hackers that some lazy programmers were taking advantage of the fact that they could use variables in PHP without defining them first. For example, they might have a variable called something like `$adminaccess` used to prevent unauthorized access from certain code, like this:

```
if ($adminaccess)
{
    // Access to sensitive functions
}
```

Elsewhere in the code there might be a statement along the lines of:

```
if ($username == 'Admin' && $password == 'secret')
    $adminaccess = 1;
```

Now, normally this would mean that only once a Username and Password had been correctly verified would `$adminaccess` be set to 1. And if they were not verified then `$adminaccess` would have no value (having not been set) and so would not have the value 1. So this would prevent unauthorized access. Or would it?

You see, nowhere in this example is `$adminaccess` initialized to 0. And if `register_globals` is set to on, then it only takes a malicious hacker to post the field name of `adminaccess` with a value of 1, and then the variable `$adminaccess` will be created by PHP and initialized with that value, opening up the sensitive code section to the hacker.

Of course a hacker would have to know the names of the variables in your code. But in well-distributed programs where the source code was known, it was easy to find omissions like this and create hacks to take advantage of them. This is why `register_globals` was set to be off by default in version 4.2 of PHP, then in version 5.3 it was deprecated, until it was finally removed altogether in version 5.4.

Note: Let this serve as a warning to you that you should always define any variable you use before it is first accessed. You never know, the server your code runs on may have an old version of PHP and your code could therefore be vulnerable to this hack. What's more, pre-defining all your variables is good practice as it helps you (and other people) better maintain you code, because you can see at a glance all the variables being used – especially if you document each too.

Redisplaying a Form

Having the form HTML and the processing code in the same PHP file makes it easy for your code to process the data received and resubmit the form (or parts of it) if any day is missing or invalid. It can also prepopulate any valid data to save the user having to type it in again.

The following revision of the earlier example (just the PHP portion, as the surrounding HTML remains unchanged) shows how to do this by allowing you to keep posting the form back to the PHP program, which pre-populates the fields with the data previously posted to it:

```php
<?php
    $username = isset($_POST['username']) ?
      $_POST['username'] : $_GET['username'];
    $password = isset($_POST['password']) ?
      $_POST['password'] : $_GET['password'];

    echo "<form method='post' action='simpleform.php'>";
    echo "Enter Username: <input type='text'    name='username' ";
    echo "value='$username' />\n";
    echo "Enter Password: <input type='password' name='password' ";
    echo "value='$password' />\n";
    echo "<input type='submit' /></form>";
?>
```

Figure 13-2 shows what this code looks like when displayed in a browser. The first difference in this code is the incorporation of the two statements to extract the posted data (which can be form either a Get or a Post request). These are the same as previously detailed.

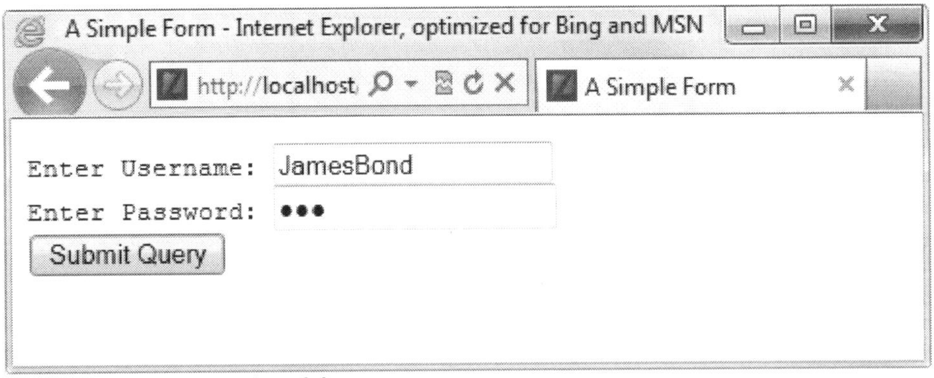

A Simple Form - Internet Explorer, optimized for Bing and MSN

http://localhost   A Simple Form

Enter Username: JamesBond

Enter Password: •••

Submit Query

Figure 2: A pre-populated form.

Then each of the two `<input>` tags has a new argument called `value`, which is given the value in either `$username` or `$password`. Because the HTML is output in double-quoted strings, it's a simple matter to place the variables directly in the strings, and their values will then be substituted by PHP (as they would if the Heredoc format is used).

You can also use the value argument to offer default values to your users. For example, if you create a loan repayment calculator most mortgages tend to be offered over 25 years, so you might choose to make that a default value, to save the user typing it in. But, being in a user-editable field, it can be easily changed if the use wants to enter a different value.

The `checkbox` and `select multiple` Input Types

There are other types of `<input />` tag you will need to be able to process from PHP, which are `checkbox`, and `select` with `multiple` enabled. These types of input arrives at a PHP server in an array because it is legal HTML to create multiple checkboxes or select lists using the same name, but with different values. For example, you might ask a user for their favorite foods out of a selection, like this:

```
Hamburger <input type='checkbox' name='foods' value='burger'  />
    Pizza <input type='checkbox' name='foods' value='pizza'   />
  Burrito <input type='checkbox' name='foods' value='burrito' />
```

Being checkboxes none, one, or some of the boxes can be checked by the user and, once you have extracted it from either the `$_GET[]` or `$_POST[]` array, you will need to access the data posted as an array, like this:

```
foreach($foods as $food) echo "You like $food<br />";
```

Or, instead of simply displaying the values in the elements of the array you can do whatever else you need to do with these values, such as processing them individually, like this:

```
$firstfood = $food[0];
```

Note: *Radio button values do not get passed in an array (and can be treated as regular form input) because only one can be selected in any group.*

Likewise, when a type of `select` is used with the option `multiple` enabled, an array will also be posted to PHP, as with this HTML:

```
Vegetables <select name="veggies" size="5" multiple="multiple">
  <option value="Peas">Peas</option>
  <option value="Beans">Beans</option>
  <option value="Carrots">Carrots</option>
  <option value="Cabbage">Cabbage</option>
  <option value="Broccoli">Broccoli</option>
</select>
```

And you could iterate through the array in a similar manner to the previous example, like this:

```
foreach($veggies as $veg) echo "You like $veg<br />";
```

Using Hidden Fields

A great way of helping a user navigate through more than one page of input (perhaps as part of an online shopping website), is to track the user by placing one or more hidden fields in a form. This lets you keep track of items already in their basket and/or any other data they may have entered, but which you don't need to confuse the user with by continually displaying.

To do this simply prepopulate a field with a `value` of your choice and give it a `type` of `hidden`, like this:

```
<input type='hidden' name='purchases' value='11324,6463,921' />
```

In this instance the `value` argument has three numbers in it, which represent inventory ID numbers of goods so far ordered by the user. When the form that this input is part of is posted back to the server with any additional item(s) to purchase, the existing items will also be posted for PHP to keep track of the order, without (yet) having to save any data to disk or a database.

Sanitizing Input

In your code that extracts form data form the `$_GET[]` or `$_POST[]` arrays it will pay you to insert some extra security to prevent malicious hacking attempts. For example, suppose you have created a bulletin board program in PHP and use it to accept input from your users, which you then display on the board.

Well, this may seem quite a simple thing to do – just accept the input and then echo it to the browser – but what if the user has entered some HTML of their own, which totally messes up the display? Or, worse still, what if they entered some JavaScript that hijacks the page and redirects the user to a different website, for example?

Obviously you can't allow that, so your best safety measure is to run all user input through the `htmlentities()` function. This takes the string that is passed to it and replaces all characters that could be interpreted by HTML with simple entities. For example, the < and > characters, which could be used to enter HTML tags, are replaced with `&lt;` and `&gt;`. This renders them harmless, but still allows < and > to be displayed in the browser.

In the same way all & characters are replaced with `&amp;` and all single and double quotes are replaced with `&#039;` and `&quot;`, along with any other characters that have equivalent HTML entities.

The end result is that a string such as `<h1>"Hello"</h1>` will be changed to `&lt;h1 &gt;&quot;Hello&quot;&lt;/h1&gt;`. This will display in the browser as typed in by the user, and not as an `<h1>` heading.

Therefore I recommend that after the two lines I introduced near the start of this lecture for extracting the Username and Password, you should now add these two lines:

```
$username = htmlentities($username);

$password = htmlentities($password);
```

Uploading Files To a Server

Uploading files to PHP is almost as simple as sending plain data. The trick is to use a special type of encoding called `multipart/form-data`; your browser will then know what to do with it, and so will PHP.

The following example enables the uploading of an image to PHP:

```
<!DOCTYPE html>
<html>
  <head>
    <title>File Upload</title>
  </head>
  <body>
    <form method='post' action='fileupload.php'
                    enctype='multipart/form-data'>
      Choose File: <input type='file' name='filename' size='27' />
      <input type='submit' value='Upload' />
    </form>
<?php
    if ($_FILES)
    {
      $name = $_FILES['filename']['name'];
      move_uploaded_file($_FILES['filename']['tmp_name'], $name);
      echo "Uploaded image '$name'<br /><br /><img src='$name' />";
    }
?>
  </body>
</html>
```

There are two parts to this example. The first contains all the HTML for setting up a web page, along with a form for selecting and uploading an image. The second part of the example is the PHP that processes the uploaded image, and you can see the result of running the code in a web browser in Figure 13-3.

The way the example works is that a form type of `multipart/form-data` is specified, along with an `<input />` type of `file`, so that a Browse button is displayed alongside, with which a file can be located on the local file system. When the form is submitted the form data is posted to the file *fileupload.php*.

In the PHP section an array called `$_FILES[]` is tested in the first line. If it has no value then no file was posted to the program, otherwise `$_FILES['filename']['name']` contains the name that was used when the file was selected by the user.

At this point, though, the file is held in a temporary storage area so next it is moved to a permanent location, using the file name just obtained:

```
move_uploaded_file($_FILES['filename']['tmp_name'], $name);
```

The value `'tmp_name'` is a temporary name that uploaded files are first given by PHP, and the `move_uploaded_file()` function copies this file to the current folder (or a subfolder or other location) as specified in the final parameter, which in this case is simply the filename in `$name`. To move the file to `/usr/home/robin` (for example) on a Linux computer you might use the following statement instead (assuming that directory exists and PHP has permission to write to it):

```
move_uploaded_file($_FILES['filename']['tmp_name'],
    "/usr/home/robin/$name");
```

However, in this example I simply have the file copied into the current folder so that it can be quickly displayed by the final line of code:

```
echo "Uploaded image '$name'<br /><br /><img src='$name' />";
```

Figure 3: Uploading a file to the web server.

The $_FILES[] Array

The $_FILES[] array can contain five different things after a file upload, as follows:

- $_FILES['file']['name'] The name of the uploaded file.
- $_FILES['file'][type'] The content type of the uploaded file (such as image/png).
- $_FILES['file']['size'] The file size in bytes.
- $_FILES['file']['tmp_name'] The name of the temporary file on the server.
- $_FILES['file']['error'] Any error code resulting from the upload.

Using these values you will know what the file was called when selected by the user, the type the file is (image, video and so on), how big it is, its temporary name on the server, and any error that may have occurred.

Some of the file types (also known as MIME types) you may encounter include the following:

- Applications: `application/pdf`, `application/zip`

- Audio: `audio/mpeg`, `audio/x-wav`

- Images: `image/gif`, `image/jpeg`, `image/png`, `image/tiff`

- Text: `text/html`, `text/plain`, `text/xml`

- Video: `video/mpeg`, `video/mp4`, `video/quicktime`

File Security

There is potential for a hacker to seriously mess up your server using file uploading unless you are careful. The way they could do this is by entering a special filename for the uploaded file, such as (for just one example) `C:/Windows/System32/calc.exe` which, on a Windows computer could replace your calculator with a malicious program!

Therefore, the example as I have written it is unsafe and it needs any characters other than alphanumeric characters and the period stripped out before being used, by replacing this line of code:

```
$name = $_FILES['filename']['name'];
```

With the following:

```
$name = strtolower(ereg_replace("[^A-Za-z0-9.]", '',
    $_FILES['filename']['name']));
```

This uses the `ereg_replace()` function (similar to `preg_replace()` as described in Lecture 12) , along with a regular expression, and uses a replacement value of the null string to remove any unwanted characters, rendering the filename safe to use.

Enclosing the name conversion code is a call to `strtolower()` which sets the resulting filename to all lower case, so that it will work on all file systems, whether case-sensitive or not. However, there's a lot more to dealing with files than this, so in Lecture 14 I cover file handling in greater depth.

Summary

You will now be able to use web forms to post data to PHP programs using either the Post or Get methods, and will be able to process the data received, whether in single values or arrays, and will be able to sanitize the input received to make it safe to work with. You also now know how to upload any type of file to PHP without creating a security risk.

In the following and final lecture we'll move onto some more advanced aspects of PHP including using cookies, file handling and communicating with JavaScript in a user's browser using Ajax.

ADVANCED PHP

By following this lecture you will:

✓ *Discover how to use cookies and sessions.*

✓ *Understand how to create, Modify and delete files.*

✓ *Learn how to perform background Ajax communication.*

Your journey to become a master PHP programmer is almost complete, but there are just a few odd bits and pieces I still have to tell you about in this final lecture – sort of the icing on the cake of PHP.

These include how to save cookies on your user's computers to personalize their browsing experience on your web pages, how to get useful information from the browser's environment, and how to provide background Ajax communication with a web server – so I'll even show you a little bit of JavaScript (not too much though).

Using Cookies

Cookies are those little snippets of data that get saved on your computer and which everyone makes such a fuss about because some companies use them to track your surfing and buying habits. However cookies are extremely useful and, in fact, invaluable for making your users' visits to your web pages as smooth and enjoyable as possible.

You see cookies are the means used by sites like Facebook and Twitter to keep you logged in, so that you can keep going back without having to continually re-enter your username and login details. And I'll now show you how easy it is for you to set and read cookies using PHP, so that you can provide the same functionality.

Cookies are sent to (and retrieved from) a web browser in header messages that get sent before a page is sent to the browser. Therefore you must always ensure that your cookie accessing takes place before a web page loads. Otherwise, if even one character of a web page has already been sent to a browser by your PHP script, then the cookie text will be treated as part of the web document, and it will therefore not work as a cookie.

Setting a Cookie

To create a cookie you simply assign it a value that contains the various details it needs to store on the user's computer. These include the cookie name, its contents, its expiry date, the domain to which it applies, the path to the server issuing it and whether it is secure or not, as follows:

- `name` The name of the cookie as used by your PHP code to access the cookie on subsequent browser requests.

- `value` The value of the cookie (the cookie's contents). It can hold up to 4KB of alphanumeric text.

- `expire` (optional – the default is that the cookie expires when the browser closes) Unix timestamp of the expiration date. Most easily set in an expression using `time()` plus a number of seconds.

- `path` (optional – the default is the current directory) The path of the cookie on the server. If this is a `/`, the cookie is available over the entire domain. If it is a subdirectory, the cookie is available only within that subdirectory.

- `domain` (optional – the default is all domains and subdirectories of the current server) The Internet domain of the cookie. If this is `myserver.com`, the cookie is available to all of `myserver.com` and its subdomains, such as `www.myserver.com` and `sport.myserver.com`. If it is a subdomain such as `sport.myserver.com`, the cookie is available only to `sport.myserver.com` and its subdomains such as `tennis.sport.myserver.com`, but not to any other main subdomains such as `news.myserver.com`.

- `secure` (optional – the default is `FALSE`) If `TRUE` the cookie must use an `https://` secure connection.

- `httponly` (optional – the default is `FALSE`) If `TRUE` the cookie must use the `HTTP` protocol – therefore cookies set in PHP will not be retrievable from JavaScript. Additionally, this setting may not be supported in all browsers, so I recommend you don't use it.

The `name`, `value` and `expire` arguments should now be quite clear but let me expand on the optional `path` argument. Don't supply an argument (or pass `''`) if you want cookies to apply in the current directory or deeper. Or you can give a value of `'/'` for the cookie to apply across all directories on the server. Or supply the location of another subdirectory, such as `'/login/'` and cookies will apply on in that directory or deeper.

The same goes for the optional `domain` argument. Don't supply an argument (or pass `''`) for the cookie to apply to the entire domain of the website. Otherwise specify a subdomain such as `'subdomain.mysite.com'` to restrict access to the cookie to that domain only.

Finally, if you have a secure web server running and wish to restrict cookie exchanges to use the SSL protocol, then set the optional `secure` argument to `'secure'`, otherwise don't pass an argument.

Therefore, to simply set a cookie's value and expiry, and have it apply only in the current folder or deeper of the current website, you might issue a simple statement such as this:

```
setcookie('username', 'FJones', time() + 60 * 60 * 24 * 7);
```

The cookie set by this assignment will have the name `username`, and the value `FJones`. It will stay on the user's computer (unless manually removed) for a week, as calculated by multiplying 60 seconds by 60 minutes, then by 24 hours, and then by 7 days. Alternatively a pre-calculated numeric value (in this case 604800) can be supplied.

Reading a Cookie

Reading back a cookie's value is simply a matter of accessing the `$_COOKIE[]` array, like this:

```
$username = isset($_COOKIE['username']) ?
  $_COOKIE['username'] : FALSE;
```

The variable `username` will now either have the value `FALSE` if the cookie was not found, or it will contain the cookie's value.

However, as previously cautioned, remember that you cannot read back a cookie's value immediately after setting it, because you can only read cookies from a web browser when they are sent to PHP as part of the header exchange prior to sending a web page to the browser.

Deleting a Cookie

To delete a cookie you simply need to use the `setcookie()` function in the same way you did to set the cookie in the first place, but with an expiry time set in the past, like this:

```
setcookie('username', '', time() - 360);
```

This function simply saves a cookie of the name `username` with no value, and sets its expiry to -360 seconds (one hour in the past), the result of which is that the cookie expires.

Note: Once you've set a cookie for a user, the next time he or she returns to your web site just check for the existence of that cookie, and if it has a value you can use it to look up their details and personalize your content for them. You can also store passwords and other values in cookies too, and the generous 4K size limit per domain means you can probably store all the cookies you could want.

Browser Identification

Even in the current times of greater browser compatibility, there still remain differences between all the major browsers, and sometimes you'll find you need to determine the user's browser in order to tailor your PHP output to provide the best possible experience. For example, it can be helpful to know if a user is browsing on a mobile device such as a phone or tablet.

To do this you can process the user agent string that the browser passes to PHP. Every web page supplies a user agent string passed to it by well-behaved browsers, and you can usually rely on this string to determine information about the user's computer and web browser. However, some browsers allow the user to modify the user agent string, and some web spiders and other 'bots' use misleading user agents, or even don't provide any user agent string.

Nevertheless, on the whole it is a very handy item of data to make use of, and takes a form such as the formidable following user agent string:

Mozilla/5.0 (compatible; MSIE 10.0; Windows NT 6.1; Trident/4.0; InfoPath.2; SV1; .NET CLR 2.0.50727; WOW64)

Each string can be different from any other due to the way the browser is configured, its brand and version, the add-ons in it, the operating system used and so on. In the instance of the preceding string it states that the browser's Internet Explorer 10, it is broadly compatible with version 5 of Mozilla based browsers such as Firefox, the operating system is Windows 7 (NT 6.1), the layout engine is Trident, .NET framework 2.0.50727 is running on the computer, and the browser is a Windows-On-Windows program (a 32-bit application running on a 64-bit processor).

Most of these you can normally ignore, but the most useful piece of information is that the browser is Internet Explorer, because sometimes you need to tailor code to specific browsers, and most frequently that has been the case with Internet Explorer – due to a history of incorporating non-standard features.

The `GetBrowser()` Function

To extract this information from the user agent string, you can use a function such as the following:

```
function GetBrowser()
{
  $UA    = $_SERVER['HTTP_USER_AGENT'];
  $agent = 'Unknown';


  if     (strstr($UA, 'MSIE'))    $agent = 'IE';
  elseif (strstr($UA, 'Opera'))   $agent = 'Opera';
  elseif (strstr($UA, 'Chrome'))  $agent = 'Chrome';
  elseif (strstr($UA, 'iPod'))    $agent = 'iPod';
  elseif (strstr($UA, 'iPhone'))  $agent = 'iPhone';
  elseif (strstr($UA, 'iPad'))    $agent = 'iPad';
  elseif (strstr($UA, 'Android')) $agent = 'Android';
  elseif (strstr($UA, 'Safari'))  $agent = 'Safari';
  elseif (strstr($UA, 'Gecko'))   $agent = 'Firefox';


  return $agent;
}
```

In this code the user agent string is retrieved from the $_SERVER[] array, and then tested for all major browsers such as Internet Explorer, Opera, Google Chrome, Apple Safari, Mozilla Firefox, Google Android, and various Apple iOS devices. The function uses the strstr() function to interrogate the user agent string, which is saved in the variable $UA. It returns the browser found (or the string 'unknown' if no browser is recognized).

So, for example, an Internet Explorer browser will return the value 'IE' when this function is called. You can test the code for yourself using the file *getbrowser.php* in the archive downloadable from the companion website.

File Handling

One of the best ways to store and retrieve large amounts of date in PHP is using the MySQL database. However, just teaching MySQL involves enough material that it would take up a separate book – in fact several books have been written on the subject.

And this is a crash course on PHP, not PHP/MySQL, so I won't digress into how you use it here. And there's no need to really, since you can perform an amazing amount of data storage and retrieval using simple flat files and the built-in PHP file handling commands.

They are fast and even support file locking to allow multiple accesses to the same file at the same time (take in turn, though, of course). In fact, to gain maximum speed, I often still stick to flat files for basic data storage as it removes all the overheads that running MySQL requires, enabling many more users to interact with the data at a time.

That said, though, once you need to start searching through data or need to perform more complicated data operations such as merging files and so on, the MySQL overheads start to outweigh the complications of convoluted file-handling functions. But for a beginner to PHP I'm sure that the following basic file-handling functions will serve all your initial needs.

First, though, a note about file naming. If you are writing code that may be used on a variety of PHP installations, there is no way of knowing in advance whether these systems are case-sensitive. For example, Windows and OS X filenames are not case-sensitive, but Linux and Unix ones are. Therefore you should always assume that the system your program is running on is case-sensitive, and therefore stick to a convention such as only allowing all lowercase filenames.

Testing For a File Existing

One of the first things you may need to do is test whether a file already exists before writing to it. Often this will be because you are going to keep updating the file, but it hasn't yet been created.

To determine whether a file exists simply call the `file_exists()` function with the filename of the file to examine, like this:

```
if (file_exists("myfile.info")) echo "File exists";
```

The `file_exists()` function returns TRUE if a file already exists, otherwise FALSE. If you don't specify a path along with the file name, the file is looked for in the current folder (the one the PHP code has been called up from). To access a different location preface the filename with a suitable path.

If your could will be distributed and therefore might be running on any of a number of platforms, you will not be able to specify an absolute path, so I recommend using relative paths, like this (not just for testing for a file's existence, but for all file operations:

```
if (file_exists("../myfiles/myfile.info")) echo "File exists";
```

If you are writing code for a particular server, though, you can use absolute paths, but I still caution you that you could well find you have to port your code at some future time, and therefore I recommend you keep these paths in global variables specified at the head of your code, like this:

```
$GLOBALS["mypath"] = '/usr/home/peter/';
```

Then whenever you access files you can attach the path like this:

```
if (file_exists($GLOBALS["mypath"] ."myfile.info"))
  echo "File exists";
```

Now, should you ever have to modify your code, all you need to do is change this and any other global path variables you have defined and it should be set to run on a new server and/or from a new location.

Note: *For the sake of brevity, the following examples will use only local file names and it is up to you to modify the code to also include paths if you intend to modify it to your own purposes.*

Creating or Opening a File

To open files for reading or writing you use the `fopen()` function and pass the file name (and optional path), along with a second argument that tells PHP how to open the file. So, to open one for writing you would use a statement such as this:

```
$filehandle = fopen('myfile.info', 'w');
```

This opens the file `myfile.info` for writing because of the `'w'` argument. A handle with which the file can be accessed while it is opened is returned by `fopen()`, and here it is saved in the variable `$filehandle`.

There are six different values you can supply to `fopen()` for specifying the way to open a file:

- `'r'` Opens a file for reading only, and places the file pointer to the start of the file. If the file doesn't exist FALSE is returned.

- `'r+'` Opens a file for reading and writing, and places the file pointer as the start of the file. If the file doesn't exist FALSE is returned.

- `'w'` Opens a file for writing only, and places the file pointer at the start of the file. If the file exists the file's length is truncated to 0. If it doesn't exist the file is created. On error FALSE is returned.

- `'w+'` Opens a file for writing and reading, and places the file pointer at the start of the file. If the file exists the file's length is truncated to 0. If it doesn't exist the file is created. On error FALSE is returned.

- `'a'` Opens the file for writing only, and places the file pointer at the end of the file. If it doesn't exist the file is created. On error FALSE is returned.

- `'a+'` Opens the file for reading and writing, and places the file pointer at the end of the file. If it doesn't exist the file is created. On error FALSE is returned.

Writing to a File

To write to a file that is open you use the `fwrite()` function, to which you pass the file handle that was returned by calling `fopen()`, and the data to be written, like this:

```
fwrite($filehandle, "Hello, this is a test");
```

You can write a small string (as in the preceding statement), or a very large one up to the single file length capacity of the current file system. The data written is saved in the file starting at the current file pointer location. As well as strings you can also write binary data (such as an image file) too.

If the file has only just been opened using an argument of `'r+'`, `'w'` or `'w+'` the writing will begin at the start of the file. But if it was opened using `'a'` or `'a+'` the writing will take place at the file's end (the data will be appended).

If `fwrite()` cannot write to the file it will return a value of FALSE (otherwise on success it returns TRUE), so it's always a good idea to access `fwrite()` in a manner such as the following:

```
$flag = fwrite($filehandle, "Hello, this is a test");
if (!$flag) die("Fatal error: could not write to file.");
```

The `die()` function outputs the string passed to it and then exits from PHP, so it's equivalent to the following but is simpler and more compact:

```
echo "Fatal error: could not write to file.";
exit;
```

You would probably use better error handling than this, by the way, but you get the picture.

Closing a File

To close a file when you have finished accessing it, you issue a call to `fclose()`, passing it the file handle, like this:

```
fclose($filehandle);
```

This will flush any as yet unwritten data to the file and then close it. After that point, `$filehandle` will be invalid unless that variable is used again when opening another file.

Reading From a File

A file that has been opened in one of the modes that supports reading can be read from in different ways. Firstly you can read in a single character using `fgetc()`, like this:

```
$ch = fgetc($filehandle);
```

This will advance the file pointer by 1 and store the character retrieved in `$ch`. But this is an unwieldy way to read from a file so there's also the `fgets()` function, which will read in a line from the file up to the next line feed character (`\n`) that it encounters, or the end of file, whichever comes first, like this:

```
$ln = fgets($filehandle);
```

If a newline is encountered it will be returned as part of the line. You can also specify a maximum number of character to read in a second argument, like this (ensuring that no more than 249 characters will be read in):

```
$ln = fgets($filehandle, 250);
```

If `fgets()` encounters an error it will return `FALSE`, so it's also a good idea to check the returned value before using it, like this:

```
$ln = fgets($filehandle, 250);
if (!ln) die("Fatal error: could not write to file.");
```

The preceding functions are handy for reading text files, but if you are reading from a binary file you will probably want to use the `fread()` function, which reads in an exact number of bytes, unless the end of file is reached, like this:

```
$data = fread($filehandle, 512);
```

This statement will read in 512 bytes from the file (or less if the end of file is reached). Should you want to read in an entire file at once you can issue a statement such as this:

```
$data = fread($filehandle, filesize($filename));
```

By using `filesize()` to return the length of the file (remembering to also enter a path, if necessary) you can quickly pull in the entire file in one go.

As with the other similar functions, if an error is encountered `fread()` will return FALSE.

Note: For very quickly grabbing the contents of a file you can use the far simpler `file_get_contents()` *function. Simply call it with the file name to read and the entire contents of that file will be returned. In fact the function is so powerful that you can also supply a URL to it and the HTML document at that URL will be returned!*

File Copying

To copy a file you don't need to open one a write another, instead there's a PHP function to do it for you called simply `copy()`. Just supply the source and destination file names (including paths as necessary), like this:

```
copy('original.file', 'copied.file') or die("Could not copy file");
```

Here you can see a new use for the `or` keyword that saves you having to use `if()` statements to check for errors. All you do after calling a function is place an `or` followed by something to do if the function returns FALSE. In this instance the `die()` function is being called. See how much simpler it is than the following:

```
$flag = copy('original.file', 'copied.file');
if (!$flag) die("Could not copy file");
```

File Deleting

To delete a file you use the `unlink()` function, like this:

```
if (!unlink('original.file')) die("Could not delete file");
```

This statement also shows another way of catching an error returned by such a function an dealing with it. In this case the returned value is directly tested by prefacing the function call with a ! operator. It's not quite as elegant as using `or` after the function, but it's another method you can choose to use.

Note: Beware that if you are calling unlink() *based on user input, you have sanitized the input sufficiently that you won't be deleting something on your server that you shouldn't be.*

File Moving

You can always move the original file after making a copy if you no-longer need it, but it's probably quicker and simpler to simply move a file using the rename() function, like this:

```
rename('original.file', 'copied.file') or die("Cannot rename.");
```

Like the other functions, if the file cannot be removed then FALSE is returned.

Random Access

Using the file pointer that every open file has you can move about within files. This gives you what is called random access to the file, in which you can move the file pointer wherever you like to read in and (if the file was opened in the right way) write out data too.

To move a file's pointer you use the fseek() function, which you pass the file handle, an offset value, and (optionally) an argument that specifies where the seek should be from. For example, to seek all the way back to the start of a file you would issue this call:

```
fseek($filehandle, 0);
```

This is directly equivalent to using the rewind() function, like this:

```
rewind($filehandle)
```

There are three optional values you can supply as a third argument to fseek(), as follows:

- SEEK_SET Seeks from the file's start.
- SEEK_CUR Seeks from the current file pointer.
- SEEK_END Seeks from the file's end.

Of these SEEK_SET is the default so the following are equivalent to each other:

```
fseek($filehandle, 0);
fseek($filehandle, 0, SEEK_SET);
```

So, to move the file pointer to the end of a file, you would use this statement:

```
fseek($filehandle, 0, SEEK_END);
```

When using the default or SEEK_SET you must use positive seek values to seek forwards into the file. Likewise, when using SEEK_END you must use negative values to seek backwards from the end. And when you use SEEK_CUR you can use either negative or positive values to seek from the current file pointer location either backwards or forwards in a file.

When you need to determine where the file pointer is in a file call the ftell() function, like this:

```
$filepointer = ftell($filehandle);
```

Note: If you have opened the file in append ('a' or 'a+') mode, any data you write to the file will always be appended, regardless of the file position, and the result of calling fseek() *will be undefined.*

Writing to a File

To write to a file you use the fwrite() function, which takes a file handle, the data to write, and (optionally) the length of data to write, like this:

```
fwrite($filehandle, $string);
```

If a length argument is given, writing will stop after the number of bytes specified have been written, or the end of string is reached, whichever comes first. So the following will write a maximum of 64 bytes:

```
fwrite($filehandle, $string, 64);
```

The writing always takes place at the current file pointer position, which then gets updated after the write to the next location following the data that was just written.

If fwrite() fails it returns FALSE, otherwise it returns the number of bytes that were written. The second argument doesn't necessarily have to be string; you can also supply binary data too.

Managing Directories

To create a new directory (assuming PHP has the correct permission in the file system to do so) you call the mkdir() function, like this:

```
mkdir('newfolder');
```

This will create a new directory called 'newfolder' in the current directory. Include a path with the file name if you need a directory created elsewhere. Upon error this function returns FALSE.

On a Unix/Linux system the default file mode for the directory will be 777, which means full access for all users. This is not very secure so you can restrict the mode with a second argument, like this:

```
mkdir('newfolder', 0755);
```

To erase a directory use the rmdir() function, like this (along with any path as necessary):

```
rmdir('newfolder');
```

Note: *Again, be careful if you are creating and/or deleting folders based on user input.*

File Locking

PHP has a built-in locking mechanism you can call on so that multiple users can access the same file at the same time, but via a queuing system so that each one gets access to the file in turn.

One reason you might do this would be, for example, to update a guestbook with comments from your users. Without locking, if two users clicked Submit at precisely the same time, it's quite likely that only one comment would get posted. But worse than that, if two PHP scripts had the file open at the same time, it could even become corrupted.

So file locking as an absolutely must-have feature on multi-user websites. To implement file locking you use the `flock()` function in conjunction with the other file system function, like this:

```php
$filehandle = fopen("guest.book", 'a+') or die("Cannot open file");

if (flock($filehandle, LOCK_EX))              // Request lock
{
  $flag = fwrite($filehandle, $comment);    // Write to file
  flock($filehandle, LOCK_UN);              // Release lock

  if (!$flag) die("Cannot write to file"); // Must be after unlock
}

fclose($filehandle);
```

In this example the file `'guest.book'` is opened for appending to. This places the file pointer at the file's end ready for writing. If the opening didn't fail the `flock()` function is called, passing it the file handle of the newly-opened file, along with a value of LOCK_EX, which means lock the file exclusively.

This places a request to PHP saying "Please give me exclusive access to this file", and the `flock()` then waits patiently in any queue of similar requests until its turn comes up, and only then it will return, releasing access to the file.

Upon returning from `flock()` the PHP code knows it now has exclusive access to the file and so it writes out the contents of `$comment` to the file (or quits with an error message if that fails).

Once the file has been written to the code calls `flock()` once more, but this time with a value of LOCK_UN which tells PHP that it has finished with its exclusive access to the file and that PHP can now assign it to the next script (if any) waiting in the queue.

The initial `flock()` call is placed within an `if()` statement because some file systems (such as FAT – particularly Windows 98) do not support file locking and so it's a good idea to see whether or not you actually achieved a secure lock before trying to write to a file. In this case, if the attempted locking fails, program flow will fall through to the `fclose()` statement and nothing with be written to the file. This is better than possibly having corrupted files.

If you plan to use code such as this you should probably consider placing a matching set of `else` statements after the `if()` to try another means of safely saving the file (or at least offering an error message to the user).

Note: For maximum response time and minimum disruption to other waiting scripts, you should only lock a file exclusively immediately before you intend to access it., You should then release the lock as soon as possible after that. Any unnecessary delays between locking a file and releasing it will mount up on a busy system and make it quite sluggish. Also, never forget to close a file lock when you have finished with it or you'll very quickly grind a server to a halt as all the requests back up.

The complete list of PHP file-handling functions (of which there are dozens) can be found here:

```
php.net/manual/en/ref.filesystem.php
```

Authentication

Using HTTP authentication you can prevent access to certain areas of a website to unauthorized users. To do this you maintain a list of valid usernames and passwords that are accepted by the server, and then add some code to your PHP that requests identification before granting access.

Let's start using an example where only one person, the administrator, is granted access, like this (see Figure 14-1):

Figure 1: Authenticating a user browsing with Internet Explorer.

```php
<?php
$username = 'admin';
$password = 'password';


if (!isset($_SERVER['PHP_AUTH_USER']) ||
    !isset($_SERVER['PHP_AUTH_PW']))
{
  header('WWW-Authenticate: Basic realm="Restricted Section"');
  header('HTTP/1.0 401 Unauthorized');
  die ("Please enter your username and password");
}
else
{
  if ($_SERVER['PHP_AUTH_USER'] != $username ||
      $_SERVER['PHP_AUTH_PW']   != $password)
```

```
        die("Invalid username/password combination");
    }
    ?>


    <!DOCTYPE html>
    <html>
      <head>
        <title>HTTP Authentication</title>
      </head>
      <body>
        <h2>Welcome. You are now logged in</h2>
      </body>
    </html>
```

Here the variables $username and $password are given values and then the global array, $_SERVER[], is tested to see whether both 'PHP_AUTH_USER' and 'PHP_AUTH_PW' have been entered by the user. If they haven't, then the following statements are executed. These send headers to the browser that will request a username and password.

Otherwise, if a username and password have been submitted, the ones received are checked against those stored in $username and $password. If they are not the same the program exits with a suitable error message. But if they do match, then program flow drops through to the HTML below to take over (or you could have more PHP code after the if() … else and it would fall through to that.

Once a user has been authenticated they can revisit the same page and, as long as they have not restarted their browser, should be able to access the page without re-authenticating.

If you try this code out on a local server through localhost you may not have the right permission set in your browser for this code to work. But you will find it works fine on any production webserver, as you can verify by testing it out on the companion website, here:

    phpcrashcourse.net/auth.php

Note: Using the file-handling functions you could easily extend this code to support additional username/password pairs, which you could check against those input over HTTP authentication. I leave that as an exercise for you to practice your new PHP skills on.

Using Sessions

Sessions are a method with which you can maintain a set of variables across multiple page loads for a user. Sessions are stored by default in special cookies in the user's browser, but if cookies are disabled they will be saved in the query string attached to the URL of subsequent web pages.

Because cookies are the most likely means of maintaining a session, you must start your session before any part of a web page has yet been output to the web browser, like this:

```
session_start();
```

Then you can store and retrieve session values using the $_SESSION[] array, like this:

```
$_SESSION['username'] = $username;
$_SESSION['password'] = $password;
```

Once you have set these session variables they will maintain their values throughout the user's current session on your site, and you can access these values from other web pages as long as you call session_start() before doing so (and before any part of the web page has been output) like this:

```
session_start();
$username = $_SESSION['username'];
$password = $_SESSION['password'];
```

You can also store other pieces of information in a session such as any other user details (like their email address), and products they have in a shopping cart, and so on.

Closing a Session

To close a session you need to reset the $_SESSION[] array so that it is empty, and remove any cookies. The following function will do all that's needed for you:

```
function CloseSession()
{
  $_SESSION = array();
  if (session_id() != "" || isset($_COOKIE[session_name()]))
    setcookie(session_name(), '', time() - 3600, '/');
  session_destroy();
}
```

It empties the `$_SESSION[]` array, then uses the `session_name()` function to find the name of the current session (if there is one), which is then removed from the user's computer by saving a new cookie of the same name, but with an expiry date and time of on hour in the past. Finally the `session_destroy()` function is called to clean everything up.

Between all these things you can be sure that a session is completely closed. But you must ensure you call the function prior to outputting any part of the HTML page.

Session Security

There is a hack whereby a malicious user will log-in to a website so that a session gets started, and make sure they have cookies disabled so that the session ID gets displayed in the address bar where they can see it. Then they may pass this URL on via spam or social networking sites in the hope that someone will click it.

If someone does click, they could find themselves inheriting the malicious person's session, and might even enter sensitive details about themselves that also gets stored in the session. And if the hacker then comes back and also enters that URL they might be able to retrieve those details.

To prevent this possibility, when you first create a session for a user I recommend you also save a copy of that user's IP address and their User Agent string, saving them as session variables. Having done that, on each new page load you can check the user's IP and User Agent against those in the session. If they match, then all's well and good. If not, then something funny's going on and you can close the session immediately.

Here's how to add those to items of data to a session:

```
$_SESSION['ip'] = $_SERVER['REMOTE_ADDR'];

$_SESSION['ua'] = $_SERVER['HTTP_USER_AGENT'];
```

Now, each time you load in session variables you can perform a quick security check at the same time, like this:

```
session_start();


if (($_SESSION['ip'] != $_SERVER['REMOTE_ADDR']) ||

  ($_SESSION['ua'] != $_SERVER['HTTP_USER_AGENT'])

{

  CloseSession();

  // Code here to open a new session

}
```

In this code a session is started (before outputting any part of the web page to the browser), and then the first thing after that is a test to see whether the save User Agent string and IP numbers match those for the current browser. If not, the `CloseSession()` function in the previous section is called, and then you need to place code of your own to open a brand new session for this user. Perhaps with a message saying "Sorry you were logged out, please sign in again" or something similar.

Note: An alternative is to require your users to allow cookies from your site (not an unreasonable request on a shopping or similar site) and force sessions to only use cookies by issuing the statement: `ini_set('session.use_only_cookies', 1);`. *Now you will not need to keep checking for session-hacking.*

Ajax With JavaScript and PHP

Ajax is the power behind what came to be known as Web 2.0. It transformed the Internet because it replaced static pages that had to be posted using forms to make changes, with much simpler behind the scenes communication with a web server – so that you merely had to type on a web page for that data to get sent to the server. Likewise, Ajax-enabled sites offer assistance whenever you needed it, for example by instantly telling you whether a username you desire is available, before you submit your signup details.

The term Ajax actually stands for Asynchronous PHP and XML. However, nowadays it almost never uses XML because Ajax can communicate so much more than that particular markup language. For example it can transfer images and videos or other files.

Initially, writing Ajax code was considered a black art that only the most advanced programmers knew how to implement. But it's not actually the case. Ajax is relatively straight-forward. However, it does require you to use JavaScript. If you are not already used to working with JavaScript then you may wish to leave this section until such time as you are ready (if you are interested, *Robin Nixon's JavaScript Crash Course* is also available from Nixon Publishing).

Creating an Ajax Object

The first thing you need to do in order to communicate with a web server via Ajax is to create a new JavaScript object, as performed by the following `CreateAjaxObject()` function:

```
function CreateAjaxObject(callback)
{
  try
  {
    var ajax = new XMLHttpRequest()
  }
  catch(e1)
  {
    try
    {
      ajax = new ActiveXObject("Msxml2.XMLHTTP")
    }
    catch(e2)
    {
      try
      {
        ajax = new ActiveXObject("Microsoft.XMLHTTP")
      }
```

```
      catch(e3)
      {
        ajax = false
      }
    }
  }


  if (ajax) ajax.onreadystatechange = function()
  {
    if (this.readyState    == 4    &&
        this.status        == 200 &&
        this.responseText != null)
      callback.call(this.responseText)
  }
  else return false

  return ajax
}
```

Let's break this down, because it's quite long but actually easy to understand. To start with the `CreateAjaxObject()` function accepts the argument `callback`, which I'll explain shortly, then a sequence of `try` and `catch()` keywords attempt to use three different methods to create a new Ajax object in `ajax`.

The reason for this is that different versions of Microsoft's Internet Explorer Browser use different methods for this, while all other browsers use yet another method. The upshot of the code is that if the browser supports Ajax (which all major modern browsers do) then a new object called `ajax` is created.

In the second part of the function there's a pair of nested `if()` statements. The outer one is entered only if the `ajax` object was created, otherwise `false` is returned to signal failure. On success an anonymous function is attached to the `onreadystatechange` event of the `ajax` object:

```
ajax.onreadystatechange = function()
```

This event is triggered whenever anything new happens in the Ajax exchange with the server. So, by attaching to it, the code can listen in and be ready to receive any data sent to the browser by the server:

```
if (this.readyState    == 4    &&
     this.status       == 200 &&
     this.responseText != null)
  callback.call(this.responseText)
```

Here the attached function checks the readyState property of the this keyword (which represents the ajax object), and if it has a value of 4 then the server has sent some data. If that's the case then if this.status has a value of 200 then the data sent by the server was meaningful and not an error. Finally if this.responseText doesn't have a value of null then the data was not just an empty string, so the callback.call() method is called:

```
callback.call(this.responseText)
```

I mentioned callback at the start of this explanation. It is the name of a function passed to the CreateAjaxObject() function, so that CreateAjaxObject() can call callback() when new Ajax data is received. The callback() function takes the value received in this.responseText, which is the data returned by the web server. I'll explain what goes into the callback() function a little later.

The PostAjaxRequest() Function

You will never have to call CreateAjaxObject() yourself because there are two more functions to complete the Ajax process (which will do the calling of CreateAjax Object() for you): one for communicating with the server by Post requests, and the other for using Get requests.

The PostAjaxRequest() function takes three arguments, the name of your callback function to receive data from the server, a URL with which to communicate with the server, and a string containing arguments to post to the server. It looks like this:

```
function PostAjaxRequest(callback, url, args)
{
    var contenttype = 'application/x-www-form-urlencoded'
    var ajax        = new CreateAjaxObject(callback)
    if (!ajax) return false


    ajax.open('POST', url, true)
    ajax.setRequestHeader('Content-type',   contenttype)
    ajax.setRequestHeader('Content-length', args.length)
    ajax.setRequestHeader('Connection',     'close')
    ajax.send(args)
    return true
}
```

What this function does is first set `contenttype` to a string value that enables encoded form data to be transmitted:

```
var contenttype = 'application/x-www-form-urlencoded'
```

Then, either the new `ajax` object is created, or `false` is returned to indicate an error was encountered:

```
var ajax = new CreateAjaxObject(callback)
if (!ajax) return false
```

Now that an `ajax` object has been created, the following lines open the Ajax request with a call to the `open()` method of the `ajax` object, send headers to the server via a Post request, including the `contenttype` string, the length of the `args` argument, and a header ready to close the connection:

```
ajax.open('POST', url, true)
ajax.setRequestHeader('Content-type',   contenttype)
ajax.setRequestHeader('Content-length', args.length)
ajax.setRequestHeader('Connection',     'close')
```

The data is then sent, the connection is closed, and a value of `true` returned to indicate success:

```
ajax.send(args)
return true
```

The `GetAjaxRequest()` Function

The `PostAjaxRequest()` function comes with a sister function that performs exactly the same process, but it sends the data using a Get request. You need to have both functions in your toolkit because some servers you may interact with require Post requests, and some will need Get requests for their Ajax calls.

Here's what the partner `GetAjaxRequest()` function looks like:

```
function GetAjaxRequest(callback, url, args)
{
   var nocache = '&nocache=' + Math.random() * 1000000
   var ajax = new CreateAjaxObject(callback)
   if (!ajax) return false

   ajax.open('GET', url + '?' + args + nocache, true)
   ajax.send(null)
   return true
}
```

One of the main differences between this and the `PostAjaxRequest()` function is that a variable called `nocache` is created from a random number, so that a unique value can be added to the query string sent by each Get request, which will prevent any caching the server might perform by ensuring every request sent is unique:

```
var nocache = '&nocache=' + Math.random() * 1000000
```

The next couple of lines are the same as the `PostAjaxRequest()` function. They create a new `ajax` object, or return `false` if that fails:

Figure 2: The Yahoo! homepage has been pulled in via Ajax.

```
var ajax = new CreateAjaxObject(callback)
if (!ajax) return false
```

Finally the Get request is made with a call to the `open()` method of the `ajax` object, the request is sent, and then `true` is returned to indicate success:

```
ajax.send(null)
return true
```

The `callback()` Function

Now we are ready to create our `callback()` function that will receive the data sent back to PHP via Ajax, as follows:

```
function callback()

{

   document.getElementById('mydiv').innerHTML = this

}
```

This code supplies the value passed to the function in `this` to the `innerHTML` property of a <div> with the `id` of `'mydiv'`. All that remains to do is create the <div>, like this:

```
<div id='mydiv'></div>
```

And now we are ready to call either the `PostAjaxRequest()` or the `GetAjax Request()` function, like this:

```
PostAjaxRequest(callback, 'ajax.php', 'url=http://yahoo.com')
```

Or, like this:

```
GetAjaxRequest(callback, 'ajax.php', 'url=http://yahoo.com')
```

In either instance a program in the same folder as the calling code, called `ajax.php`, is chosen for the communication, and the URL `'http://yahoo.com'` is sent to the program as the value of the key `url`.

The *ajax.php* Program

The last part of the Ajax puzzle is to write the program that will reside on the web server and communicate with the web browser, and that's this short snippet of PHP:

```
echo isset($_POST['url']) ?
   file_get_contents($_POST['url']) :
   file_get_contents($_GET['url']);
```

What it does is test whether the key `url` has been sent to it, either in a Post request (as `$_POST['url']`), or in a Get request (as `$_GET['url']`). In either case the PHP `file_get_contents()` function is called on the value passed to it (which in this case is `'http://yahoo.com'`). This fetches the web page referred to, which is then returned to the calling Ajax function using the PHP `echo` keyword.

Figure 14-2 shows the result of running the previous Ajax example (saved as *ajax.htm* in the accompanying archive), which then communicates with *ajax.php* (also in the archive) on the web server, to insert the contents of the *Yahoo!* home page into a `<div>` element.

For ease-of-access I have saved the three Ajax functions in the file *ajaxfunctions.js* in the accompanying archive, so that you can include them in the `<head>` of any web page you create that will employ Ajax communication, like this:

```
<html>
  <head>
    <script src='ajaxfunctions.js'></script>
    <!-- etc... ->
```

Summary

And that, as they say, is that! You've reached the end of this crash course and I hope you found it as easy to follow as I promised at the start. You now have all the skills you need to be a proficient PHP programmer and are well on your way to creating popular and dynamic web sites.

Thanks for taking this course, and good luck!

- Robin Nixon

INDEX

3256589R00137

Printed in Great Britain
by Amazon.co.uk, Ltd.,
Marston Gate.